Praise

MW00633254

Repurposement

"In **Repurposement**, Troy Redstone has tackled one of the most pervasive and most ignored crises facing our nation today. Using relatable language and touching personal anecdotes, Troy is able to help us examine retirement in an unexpected and powerful new way."

Dr. Daniel Crosby
Author of **The Laws of Wealth** and **The Behavioral Investor**

"Repurposement is about achieving a timely and dignified retirement that requires a thoughtful and proactive approach to establishing goals and maximizing pre-retirement savings. Engaging an experienced retirement planning professional is the best way to ensure your path is realistic and that you stay on course."

Jason C. Roberts, ERISA Counsel
Pension Resource Institute, CEO
Retirement Law Group, Partner

"We live in vision or we live in circumstance. This incredible book by Troy helps us take a look at the circumstance of retiring and having the vision of making the following years the best years. With all the years of living and learning why waste it and just live without purpose. I use a phrase often: So What...Now What. This book teaches – So What...you retired – Now What? Be a blessing and make a difference."

Dr. Kevin Elko
Author of **The Sender, True Greatness**, and **The Pep Talk**

"I'm a firm believer in the importance of purpose in every season of our lives. Troy takes a look at the traditional idea of retirement and suggests an idea for a fuller, more impactful life – Repurposement. With Troy's book, no matter what season you're in, it's not too late to repurpose to create your best life in every way. Let's GO!"

Gregg Knapp,
National Talk Show Host and Author of **GO!**

"I want to be living when I die. My desire is to enjoy every minute of life. Repurposement is about finishing well."

Dr. Keith Newman, President, **Southern Nazarene University**

"So many people think retirement is the end, when in fact it truly is a beautiful reset. Troy's mission to help people redefine retirement is as refreshing as it is necessary in such a stressful financial climate. By helping people look past the math, *Repurposement* sets the stage for a meaningful transition into retirement."

Peter Dunn (Pete the Planner®)
USA Today Money columnist and Author of ten books

"As each of us runs our race in life, shouldn't our goal be to sprint rather than coast? Troy Redstone cheers us on and shows us that it is much better to **repurpose** than to retire."

Dr. Everett Piper, President, **Oklahoma Wesleyan University**
Author of *Not a Daycare*

"In his book, Troy hits well upon one of the most key aspects of preparing for retirement from our vocations: 'What do I do with my time and resources post-retirement to fulfill not only my needs but, potentially, the needs of others?' His idea of *Repurposement* is unique and positions the readers to positively reconsider what life can be post working career."

James D. Robison, AIF®, Founder, **White Oak Advisors**
PlanAdviser's Top 100 Retirement Plan Advisers, 2013, 2015, 2017

"Every season of life represents an opportunity. Striking the balance between today's calling and tomorrow's promise is the stuff of this book, opening eyes to the power of purpose in every season. **Repurposement** will empower you to maximize the moment so you can seize the future."

Jim Lyon, General Director, **Church of God Ministries**
Author of *Go Ahead. Ask Anything.*

"The attraction of rest after many years of productive labor is certainly understandable. But there's not much sadder than a gifted, capable leader choosing to become a mere spectator or, at most, a grumpy critic. *Repurposement* does not mean delaying retirement, but instead combining your gifts, skills, wisdom, and passion to work toward goals that truly matter."

Glenn Waddell, General Counsel and Chief Compliance Officer
EverSource Wealth Advisors® LLC

Repurposement

EXPERIENCING THE FINANCIAL FREEDOM
TO START LIVING ON PURPOSE TODAY

Troy L. Redstone

Mahout Press Inc
Made in the USA
Lexington, KY

For information about permission to reproduce selections from this book
Write to Permissions, Walsworth Publishing
306 North Kansas Avenue, Marceline, Missouri 64658

For information about special discounts for bulk purchases, please contact
Mercedes Givens at 1-844-PHD-401(k)

Manufacturing and Printing by Mahout Press, Inc.
Book design by Terry Epps
Cover photos by Linsey McAfee

Library of Congress Cataloging-in-Publication Data

Redstone, Troy L., 1967-
Repurposement: Experiencing the financial freedom
to start living on purpose today / Troy L. Redstone – First trade edition.
ISBN 978-1-7340927-0-7
I. Retirement Planning – Personal Finance / Money
II. Business & Economics – Psychological aspects / Behavioral Psychology

Mahout Press Inc

Made in the USA
Printed in Lexington, Kentucky

2 3 4 5 6 7

To my amazing bride, Kristalynn
… forever and ever, Amen.

And to the retirement plan professionals
who continue to raise the bar.
I am humbled to be part of the "fraternity"
of professional retirement plan advisors,
subject matter experts, "ERISA Geeks,"
and Plan Fiduciary Advisors.
This book is not a trumpet call to hire me –
my Marketing Director does that for me,
opening some doors and closing others.
This book is a trumpet call to find your purpose,
to seek Repurposement (a better target than retirement),
and to find a pilot to help you in your journey.

CONTENTS

FORWARD

I must admit, when Troy first mentioned he was writing a book about people being more engaged for retirement, my first reaction was possibly like some of you: "just what we need, another self-help/saving for retirement book!"

However, what I have learned over my years of knowing and working with Troy Redstone is he is unabashedly willing to take risks and reinvent ideas in innovative ways that others only catch up to later. As an example, I remember hearing Troy once speak about "Financial Wellness" at least two years before the term became a more household term in the retirement plan universe.

And so, it is no surprise really that Troy is not writing a book about each of us doing a better job to improve our financial conditions for when we retire; he is challenging us to all reach a whole new PURPOSE for WHY we retire to begin with. Only then can we truly find the motivation to save in ways we possibly never thought possible.

Using personal anecdotes, statistics and real-life examples, REPURPOSEMENT gives a completely different frame of reference beyond "saving more for retirement". Troy calls on his years of working in the pulpit, the boardroom and breakroom to help each of us to find that larger purpose for planning for the future, regardless of economic means and individual circumstances.

I invite you to REPURPOSE your life!

Brian M. Johnston
Attorney at Law
Jackson Lewis, P.C.

PREFACE

Who should read this book … and why?

This book was written to memorialize the lessons and steps for managing money, building wealth, and preparing for the future. These are lessons I have learned and stories I have shared over the last two decades.

The audience for this book is young Americans just starting to invest as well as workers who are about to retire. Eventually we will provide supplemental materials like "Repurposement for those in their 20's" and "Repurposement for those in their 50's" but the message of this book is for readers of all ages.

Fundamentally, the message of this book is intended for employees who work for an employer sponsoring a retirement plan (something like a 401k or 403b plan) as well as the employers who sponsor those plans.

This book is about how to make the 401k work.

The book involves a lot of what we might traditionally call "retirement education," though retirement education has largely failed. After dozens of years and millions of dollars invested, far too many Americans are still not investing enough. The best efforts of those in the retirement plan industry have barely moved the needle on participation rates and investment rates, the average account balance has not grown significantly, and most Americans are inadequately prepared to retire. And most employees still find their 401k plan too confusing.

Retirement education has failed.

I can say this because, as an insider, I used to be part of the problem. But I think I've discovered the solution and it is not complicated. The solution is to simplify the process and focus on holistic financial wellness. That's what this book does and that's why you should read it.

I realized the industry was making it too complicated. Employees just need a simple, how-to manual for the 401(k), without trying to sell them anything and without turning the employee meeting into "Finance 101." Retirement education which uses a lot of confusing terminology, trying to turn employees into CIOs (Chief Investment Officers) is not helpful. Employees just need to embrace their role as the CSO (Chief Savings Officer).

Half the problem was the industry had overcomplicated it.

But the other half of the problem with trying to get more Americans to invest more money is to realize some people literally can't afford to save more. This is where financial wellness comes in. A holistic approach to money management was needed to teach proper stewardship and budgeting.

The final piece which tied together the need for better education and holistic financial wellness was understanding the motivation behind why we need to prepare for the future. I realized traditional retirement education was not producing behavioral change because too few employees understood the WHY.

Repurposement is all about understanding the WHY.

It dawned on me one day the traditional concept of retirement is not very inspiring; it wasn't motivating to me or to the employees I was serving.

Retirement is this idea that if we have enough money, we can do nothing, like the Benjamin Franklin quote: "Most people die at 25 but aren't buried until they're 75."

I believe we have a savings problem in America … and a money problem and a retirement problem … because most of us haven't been given a good WHY … a good reason to invest more and make our money behave. This book talks about the WHY, which should make it an important read for everyone. It's a paradigm shift from the traditional approach.

Rather than retirement, I would like to be an advocate for Repurposement.

I'd like to encourage Americans to use the first chapter of their life, when they may be working in a job they do not find particularly purposeful or fulfilling, to prepare for the second chapter. This is what Repurposement is all about. We must be freed from this idea that retirement is an age or that it is checking out to do nothing. I am an advocate for identify our purpose and living on purpose in every chapter of life. And I am motivated about helping employees build the financial freedom for Repurposement.

This book is for every employee who wants to learn the keys to building wealth to gain financial freedom. But this book is also for the employers who sponsor those retirement plans. If the plan is working correctly, the employees can retire with dignity and be repurposed on their own terms, which benefits them. But it also benefits the employers because having employees stick around beyond their most productive years costs the company more in higher health care, higher worker's comp, and lost productivity.

Employees who care about the future should read this book.

And employers who care about their employees should read it.

And it's easy for me to get excited about helping employers who want to help their employees.

America is facing a retirement crisis. This book describes the solution. The solution begins with understanding our WHY which prepares the context for real behavioral change, and then simplifying the 401k in a how-to manual within the context of basic financial wellness.

It's not rocket science and you don't need a finance degree.

If this book is in your hands Repurposement is within your grasp.

Introduction
Why this is personal to me
The passion behind *Plan Health Design*

My passion is to serve others to help them gain the financial freedom to live the life they're called to lived. If it's not in their current job or assignment I hope to help them have the financial freedom to leave and follow their heart. I want to help people find their purpose and live on purpose and eventually to be repurposed … that is say, to be financially able to be repurposed whenever they identify their purpose.

Whether you are a young employee following your passions rather than chasing a paycheck, or a seasoned employee who gained the financial freedom to become an encore entrepreneur, I don't ever want to see someone stuck in a job because they can't afford to leave. Nor do I want to see people having to work beyond their most productive years.

Life is too short to not live on purpose.

Which is why I call it Repurposement rather than Retirement.

The Repurposement industry is the next generation of the retirement industry, fueled by a desire to help employees retire with dignity on their own terms when they're ready to move on. Previous generations may have remained in jobs because they lacked the financial freedom to leave and explore work which was more purposeful, meaningful and gratifying. But the generation currently entering the workforce has proven they will take a position for less pay if its more fulfilling.

The job of the retirement industry should be to help workers gain the financial freedom to facilitate the higher quality of life desired. But it will require a shift within the industry, from retirement education to financial education; from a focus exclusively on the retirement plan to a more holistic focus on financial wellness; and from an industry dominated by financial brokers to a discipline practiced by behavioral scientists and fee-only benefits consultants.

The point is, whether you're a new employee in your first job trying to build financial independence or a seasoned employee preparing to leave your job to become an encore entrepreneur, the retirement plan industry should promote the wellness required to be repurposed whenever you feel the call.

I felt the call some time ago, but retirement became personal to me about a dozen years ago when my own father reached this fictitious age. I have watched how it worked (or how the math didn't work) for him. And I can't help but think the path he is on now was so avoidable. His retirement outcome had much less to do with the economy or market conditions or even his income, all things beyond our control. But it had a ton to do with poor planning, or lack of planning.

My dad did not plan or prepare well for retirement, which is typical of many Americans today. But my goal is to change that and reshape a national dialogue around planning, beginning with understanding why we should plan, and what we are planning for.

Every day, about 10,000 more American workers are moving into retirement,[1] but it is a very uncertain retirement, one fraught with dangers and pitfalls, one that is only a slight misstep of health care concern away from financial catastrophe. Even those American workers who were prepared, who sat down and thought through the math, are finding the math doesn't work so well now that retirement is upon them.

To understand what happened to my dad readers probably need to understand a thing or two about him.

My dad is a big man, nearly 6'8" in his prime. He's also brilliant, the mind of an engineer, great at problem solving, never met a puzzle he couldn't figure out, whether it involved carpentry, electrical engineering, plumbing, technical wiring, aviation or automotive engineering, or anything related to a combustible engine. The mind of an engineer ... just not the engineering degree. He's extremely bright but he wasn't educated in the traditional way. Instead of going to college, he served in the Air Force. After leaving the service he worked for 40 long, hard years and retired from the only real job he ever had.

Remember when people used to write hand-written notes, back before the advent of email? The last person I remember who still participated in the ancient ritual of putting pen to paper was my grandmother, GG, who lived to be 94 years old. We could never get her to use email, but she regularly wrote personal notes, letters and cards which we now treasure in our family.

My dad is the guy who used to deliver those handwritten notes, treasures of ink and parchment. He was a mailman, a postal carrier, for forty years. He was literally and figuratively a blue-collar worker – all of his uniforms were blue. It was a respectable Civil Service job after he left the military service. He worked long, hard days, especially at Christmas, because neither snow nor rain nor heat nor gloom of night stays the swift delivery of cards from GG.[2]

As a Civil Service employee, the pay wasn't outstanding, but it was adequate, and the benefits were outstanding. The National Association of Letter Carriers provided a pension plan and since they were connected to the government there was little concern about the pension plan failing. It was a fairly simple system. A person put in their time and then the pension plan took care of them when their time was up. He kind of did some math in his head and figured he'd be fine... but somehow the math's been a little fuzzy for my dad since retirement.

Here's the point: we all know there were attorneys and actuaries and high-priced financial advisors in thousand-dollar suits who met with the trustees of the billion-dollar pension plan, but no one ever talked to my dad. The advisors and consultants never left the board room and walked out on the floor and talked to the mailmen. No one ever talked to him about how much he was saving or even the fact that he needed to invest something additional to what the pension would provide. Like a lot of people, he had a basic distrust of the stock market, so investing for him would have been like gambling. He tried not to go too much into debt, but he never invested much, never really budgeted, never really planned.

He wasn't in control of his money; it was in control of him ... or rather the creditors were.

And then there's Social Security. Today Social Security provides, on average, about a third of what retirees need to retire.[3] And if it's a third today it's unlikely to be even close to a third in the future. I am not among those who believe it will completely go away by the time I retire but I'm definitely of the opinion it will become a smaller and smaller portion of what we actually need to retire. We can all tout the failures and the shortfalls of the Social Security system, but in fairness it's actually working pretty much as it was originally designed to work.

The Social Security Act of 1935 which established the Old Age, Survivors and Disability Insurance (OASDI) program uses words like "supplemental" and "assistance." In other words, the original intent was for the government to supplement what we were doing and what our employer was doing. It was never meant to provide everything we needed in retirement. And it still supplements some of what we need, though funding for the program is beginning to dry up. When Social Security was introduced it didn't mean we were off the hook. We still had responsibility.

After all, a person can't get something for nothing ... unless they're Ida May Fuller, the very first recipient of Social Security benefits. She only paid $24.75 into the program but collected $22,888![4]

Today our responsibility and burden is greater than ever. The fact that most employers have phased out pension plans[5] and Social Security is expected to provide a smaller and smaller supplement in retirement means the burden is shifting squarely back to our portion, to our responsibility to invest more. I'd apologize for being the bearer of bad news, but a person would have to be living under a rock ... in a cave ... on Mars ... to not know this is the state of the crisis we face as a nation.

Too many Americans are stuck in jobs they can't afford to leave

Do you know how most Americans retire today? After the pensions dried up and the government dollars ran short, the increasingly common means of retiring today is getting a second job in retirement, not necessarily a job they like, doing something they like, but a job they have to have just to pay the bills. Seems like a pretty lousy definition of retirement, but it is a reality for a lot of Americans. People stay in jobs they hate because they can't afford to leave ... or they leave their job only to take a second job they like even less, to make ends meet. I call it the Wal-Mart retirement plan.

"Hi. Welcome to Wal-Mart."

When I go to Wal-Mart and see someone the age of my parents standing at the door, I always have two thoughts. My first thought is, "God bless them, I hope they're enjoying what they're doing," and every once in a while the greeters are smiling and they look as if it's not such an awful job.

But my second, almost immediate thought is, "I'll bet that's not how they pictured retirement. I'll bet they didn't work a long, hard time down at the factory or the Post Office or the plant so they could stand at the door of Wal-Mart and greet me when I came to buy my toiletries. I'll bet that wasn't their retirement dream."

When I walk into a Home Depot, for instance, I look for someone who looks *like* my dad because I hardly know which end of the hammer to hold. My dad has always been very handy and very knowledgeable on DIY projects. You name it and my dad can fix it. I'm amazed by how handy he is and equally amazed by how little of it I inherited. So I look for someone who looks *like* my dad ... but I don't really want it to be my dad. He walked a ton of miles delivering mail and I'd like for him to just be able to rest or devote his time and energy towards something which feeds his passion, whether it pays the bills or not. If he wants to work that's fine. I just don't want him to have to work.

A "have-to" job, a second job in retirement a person must have because the first job didn't fund retirement, is not anyone's retirement dream, but it is retirement reality for millions of Americans today. And it is sad because it is entirely avoidable.

I guess falling short of our retirement dreams has been growing increasingly sad for many years, but it became personal to me when it became my dad. When I look at the average employee, I see my dad, I see folks that just need someone to care enough to provide some guidance and preparation for the largest financial purchase of their lives. The owner of the company and the wealthy have their financial advisors, but the employees, the average American worker, needs help. It was for this population that the 401(k) plan[6] was created, but it was delivered without a good instruction manual.

One thing my dad and I do have in common, beyond our height, is the mindset of an engineer, always asking how things could be designed better. It started for me with a fascination about why people do the stuff they do and gradually became fascination with why people do the stuff they do with money. (Spoiler alert: the stuff people do with money is often not really smart stuff.) In fact, when money is on the table, we often toss logic aside and follow our emotions in the most irrational of ways. Dave Ramsey likes to say something along the lines of 'when our money comes out ... our stupid comes out too.'

But it doesn't have to. The engineer in me says we just need a good instruction manual.

Stupid and money don't mix well just as a fool and his money are soon parted.[7] The examples of this proverb are all around us.

With the stock market, for example, our emotions often prompt the antithesis of reasonable action. The markets rising in price ignites a buying frenzy while falling markets prompt a sell-off. If our favorite retailer announced things would be priced double this weekend, we would not rush to the store to buy things at an inflated price, but this is how we treat the stock market, which means we buy high. Conversely, when the markets fall, we're prompted by fear to sell low. But buying high and selling low is a formula for certain disaster. If a person repeats this cycle very many times they will be broke.

Another example is what I would call Confidence Bias. This is the idea that the more confident someone appears to be the more accurate their stock picks are assumed to be. The research shows the opposite to be true in many cases.

Yet another example is what I would call Optimism Bias, the irrational belief that we are less likely to experience negative events than others, or the idea that bad stuff always happens to someone else and we're surprised it happens to us. For some reason, people apply this in the world of economics disproportionately than to other arenas of life. For instance, we would never assume we could play basketball against Michael Jordan (he would crush us) but we act as if we can pit our investment prowess against Warren Buffet (or similarly competent professionals). Retirement plan participants given a choice to self-direct or use the advice of professionals often make the mistake of choosing to manage their own accounts as if they are just as smart as professional money managers.

We're not smart when it comes to money and we don't make the best decisions. Our emotions hijack the process. But I believe, with the proper education and support (reframing the dialogue) and with hands on training (and even handholding) it is possible to have enough money to retire on time and to retire with dignity (the basic definition of retirement readiness). It's not a pipedream and with a few tweaks here and there (and a few tough choices) it can be your reality. It takes time and it takes enough smarts to know what you don't know.

But it's doable. The math really works: $5,000 a year for 40 years at an 8% rate of return is not unreasonable for most people. The key is starting early enough and not giving up along the way. Every little bit helps and the sooner the better. It just takes time.

Warren Buffett was asked about the biggest mistake people make when it comes to money. He said, "Not learning the habit of saving early, and then trying to get rich quick. It's pretty easy to get well-to-do slowly. But it's not easy to get rich quick."[8]

Books titled "Get well-to-do Slowly" are not flying off the shelves at most bookstores but books which promise getting rich quick sell, which is fine ... they just need to be sold in the fiction section.

In college I studied Behavioral Psychology with an emphasis on Industrial & Organizational Psychology. I received a second degree in journalism because I enjoy writing and a graduate degree in ministry because I enjoy serving people. But increasingly I felt called to help people understand how to make better choices with money. After all, most of us don't have a very healthy relationship with money.

In all of my years traveling and speaking I discovered people tend to fall into one of two extremes in their relationship with money, regardless of where they live or in what socioeconomic bracket they reside: either they waste money or they worship it.

WASTE  WORSHIP

Most people do not hit the extreme end of the scale on either side, but fewer still are perfectly balanced in the middle.

Some of us are controlled by it, few of us master it. For me personally, I will confess my tendency is to fall towards worship, as evidenced by the fact that I worry too much about money (either I worry about how much I make to provide for my family or I worry about how much I spend). Worry is just another form of worship. The worry takes hold in my heart because the money has too much of a hold over my heart. Understanding and identifying our tendency might begin to reveal some of the emotions at play that impact our decision-making when it comes to how we handle money.

Emotions impact financial decisions, even for the most rational among us. There is little correlation sometimes between a person's education or intelligence and their ability to make sound financial decisions over time. When it comes to money our hearts are often in the way of our heads. I returned to college to pursue an MBA in Finance because Behavioral Finance is at the heart of choice architecture, helping us understand how we make financial decisions, identifying the behavioral challenges we face with money and providing real behavioral solutions ... like an instruction manual for the 401(k) plan.

Behavioral Finance is a new discipline. In 2002, behavioral psychologist Daniel Kahneman won the Nobel Prize in economics for his seminal work on behavioral economics. His work recognized the important role of emotion in decision-making. It had long been speculated emotions impact our ability to make good decisions but there was no "science" behind it prior to Kahneman's work. He was able to prove in certain circumstances we make predictable errors in judgment based on emotions.

An employer-sponsored retirement plan (like a 401k) is less an investment vehicle than it is a study in behavioral psychology because if there are a hundred participants in the plan there are at least a hundred different behavioral dynamics at work, and a hundred different opinions on how to handle money.

- If we do this how will employees respond? What if we tweak this?
- What choices can we engineer to increase savings or to produce better investment decisions?
- It's choice architecture and behavioral science, and there's no one-size-fits-all approach that works.
- Each employee population is unique, and each retirement benefit program needs to be uniquely engineered to fit the audience.

With plan health design many of the biggest behavioral challenges can be addressed with proven solutions, but there will always be challenges even with good choice architecture. The solution is broader than retirement education; it involves financial education or more accurately, financial wellness.

When the wellness movement started in 1969, Dr. Bill Hettler built the foundation of wellbeing on "Six Dimensions of Wellness" … but financial wellness was not one of his core principals. He left financial wellness out and we are still paying the price for the mistake.[9]

Consider how most people learn about money. Some learn about money from their parents, which is why the same financial mistakes are passed on from generation to generation. Others learn about money from their peers, though the "expert" at the water cooler may not be an expert, just the loudest person at work. (Let's be honest, if they were as brilliant in their investment prowess as they suppose they would probably be on Wall Street, not working there on Main Street.) Still others learned about money (the time value of money, how compound interest works, etc.) from an insurance salesman. (Might the salesman have had an ulterior motive beyond pure and simple education?)

In some states, students are required to take a class in personal finance before graduating high school. Unfortunately, in most states, kids can still leave school with no education about money and finance, zero ability to balance a checkbook and craft a budget, and completely unprepared for the onslaught of credit card companies that await them in college.

Our retirement plan is the biggest purchase we will ever make. (No, it is not our home. It is our retirement plan.) And that is if we are one of the lucky employees who has access to an employer-sponsored retirement plan. The coverage gap is even larger for this benefit than it is for health insurance. Employees can open their own IRA, of course, paying higher fees for lower contribution limits, but they are less likely to be successful if they don't have access to "savings made simple" where the money comes right out of their paycheck and into their investments before they can spend it. An IRA is a poor substitute for an employer-sponsored plan.

Participation in an employer-sponsored plan is the first big decision we'll be asked to make at work and unfortunately, it is also the most important financial decision we will ever make.

New employees (perhaps in their first job) and recent college grads (maybe still living in an apartment or living at home with their parents) are asked to make the most important purchase they will ever make.

Ever.

They probably think their really big purchase still awaits them when they buy their first home, but their biggest financial transaction was when the 401(k) enrollment form was put in front of them. And most new employees are not equipped to handle the decision. Perhaps they turned it down or chose to contribute too little, less than the company match, and the mistake won't be realized until it is so late in the game it is nearly impossible to fix. There is a huge need for financial literacy that begins with equipping employees to make their most important financial decision on Day 1 at their new job.

Former Fed Chairman Alan Greenspan was famously quoted during the economic downturn in 2008 as saying, "The number one problem in today's generation and economy is the lack of financial literacy." The economic recession revealed far too many Americans were living beyond their means. They simply lacked the basic financial literacy to handle money and make wise financial decisions so when things got tight the lack of expertise was exposed.

ERISA, which we will talk about throughout this book, is the governing legislative framework for regulating employer-sponsored benefits like a 401(k) plan. It stands for the Employee Retirement Income Security Act of 1974. In ERISA, the guidelines talk about the "Prudent Man Rule"[10] as in, "What would a prudent person, knowledgeable in such matters, choose to do in like circumstances?" In Behavioral Finance we like to refer to the "rational man"[11] as in, "What would a rational person unencumbered by emotional impulses choose to do in these circumstances?"

The problem is that the rational man does not exist. He is a fictional construct in Behavioral Finance by which we measure our irrational, impulsive financial decisions. Most of us are not prudent or rational when comes to money. Our emotions impact our wallets, our wallets expose our hearts,[12] and our hearts are sometimes miles away from our heads (not 12 inches).

Employees do not always act like the rational person any more than employers sponsoring the 401(k) plan always act like the prudent person. We are merely human, and we work for humans, fallible and prone to fairly predictable behavioral errors in judgment. Unfortunately, a mistake with the biggest financial choice of our lives could be a very costly error.

1. According to a Deutsche Bank report issued November, 2018
2. Inscribed on New York's James Farley Post Office in New York City, facing Penn Station
3. According to the Social Security Administration (www.ssa.gov) Social Security retirement benefits will replace less than 40 percent for average wage earners. The percentage is lower for people in the upper income brackets and higher for people with low incomes.
4. Ida May Fuller was very close to retirement age when Social Security was established. She only paid into the program for a few payroll cycles before retiring at age 65. Her total deposits into Social Security were $24.75 and her very first Social Security check was $22.54. At the time life expectancy was age 79, meaning she was expected to live another 14 years collecting on Social Security. The government knew she would collect much more than she deposited, a fantastic return even under normal circumstances, but her circumstances were not normal. She lived to be 100 and collected $22,888 – much, much more than they ever anticipated.
5. Only 7% of Fortune 500 companies still offered the traditional company pension plan as of 2013, according to a Towers Watson study
6. The 401(k) is a very specific type of retirement plan which derives its name from the section of Internal Revenue Code that outlines this provision. Throughout this book, however, references to 401(k) are meant to be general in nature and could apply to 401(a) plans, profit sharing plans, 403(b) plans, Governmental 457 plans, and similar employer-sponsored retirement plans.
7. Proverbs 21:20
8. Sports Illustrated, February 3, 2014, p. 25
9. Bill Hettler, MD introduced wellness around the idea of lifestyle choices, trying to bring balance by focusing on each of six dimensions of wellbeing: Emotional Wellness, Occupational Wellness, Physical Wellness, Spiritual Wellness, Intellectual Wellness, and Social Wellness. He did not include Financial Wellness, which is only recently receiving attention within the wellness movement.
10. The **Prudent Man Rule** is based on common law from the 1830 Massachusetts court case, *Harvard College v. Amory* The prudent man rule, written by Massachusetts Justice Samuel Putnam, directs trustees "to observe how men of prudence, discretion and intelligence manage their own affairs, not in regard to speculation, but in regard to the permanent disposition of their funds, considering the probable income, as well as the probable safety of the capital to be invested." Later the guideline of prudence was incorporated into ERISA 404(a)(1) as "A fiduciary shall discharge his duties with respect to a plan solely in the interest of the participants and beneficiaries and (A) for the exclusive purpose of: (i) providing benefits to participants and their beneficiaries; and (ii) defraying reasonable expenses of administering the plan: (B) with the care, skill, prudence, and diligence under the circumstances then prevailing that a prudent man acting in a like capacity and familiar with such matters would use in the conduct of an enterprise of a like character and with like aims; (C) by diversifying the investments of the plan so as to minimize the risk of large losses, unless under the circumstances it is clearly prudent not to do so; and (D) in accordance with the documents and instruments governing the plan insofar as such documents and instruments are consistent with the provisions of this title."
11. The **Rational Man,** or *homo economicus*, is a mythical construct from economic theory portrayed as a person who is consistently rational. Economists in the late 19th century built mathematical models on these economic assumptions of rationality, and by the mid-20th century, the rational choice theory of Lionel Robbins dominated mainstream economics. But empirical studies by cognitive and mathematical psychologist Amos Tversky questioned the assumption that investors are rational. Tversky was a collaborator of Daniel Kahneman, an economist notable for his work on the psychology of judgment and decision-making, as well as behavioral economics, for which he was awarded the 2002 Nobel Memorial Prize in Economic Sciences. With behavioral economists like Richard Thaler, the Rational Man was exposed as a completely mythical creature.
12. "For where your treasure is, there your heart will be also." Matthew 6:21

CHAPTER 1
CLARIFYING THE WHY
Avoiding three common mistakes with retirement savings

It is important to start building wealth by knowing our why.

Why embark on this journey, why is it worth the sacrifice and time and energy? Studies have shown employees who look at a picture of their family right before electing their contribution rate select a higher savings rate because they remind themselves why (and for whom) they save. Other studies have shown higher investment rates among employees who look at an age-progressed picture of themselves to call to mind what might be at stake.

There are a number of mistakes commonly made with 401k plans, but the biggest mistakes are errors related to the WHY.

MISTAKE #1 – NOT STARTING WITH A GOAL IN MIND

One of the biggest mistakes made with retirement plans is not starting with a clear picture of the future. It makes it impossible to keep our eyes on the prize, to finish the race in a successful fashion, or to even complete the journey. After all, if a person does not keep their eye on the prize, they are likely to give up when faced with challenges along the way.

But to be fair, it's hard to keep our eyes fixed on a goal we can't even imagine.

The 1974 UCLA Bruins were the best team in college basketball. They were incredible. The second-best team in the nation ... was the backup players on their bench. The team was that good. Their record of 11 national titles includes an amazing streak of seven in a row at one point, a feat unmatched by any team in any sport. They won the national title in 1967, 1968, 1969, 1970, 1971, 1972, and 1973. In fact, in 1974, not only had they not lost the national championship in seven years, they hadn't even lost a game in several seasons. They won 88 games in a row!

They were scheduled to play Notre Dame on January 19, 1974, and the coach for the Fighting Irish, Digger Phelps, had the monumental task of getting his team ready. It was a big task because he had to get inside his player's heads and convince them they even had a chance.

The biggest opponent they would face was their own doubts.

Coach Phelps started the week with a typical practice, just like any other practice, with one exception. At the end of practice, he had them bring out a ladder and he had his team practice cutting down the nets. Coach Phelps did it again the following day after practice and the following day after practice. By the time the ball tipped on Saturday the team could imagine what it might look like to win. With their coach's help they could visualize it. They were skilled basketball players but highly skilled net-cutters. And they had a picture of winning – once thought impossible – crystal clear in their minds.

When the final buzzer sounded, they had beaten UCLA 71-70 and ended the longest winning streak in the nation.

Reaching retirement is not impossible but as goals go ... it might be harder than beating the 1974 UCLA Bruins ... and for much of the same reasons: it is difficult for us to visualize. I believe there is a direct correlation between the detachment from our future selves and the disintegration of the extended family unit. When previous generations grew up living with aging parents and grandparents, surrounded by aunts and uncles, it was not as hard to imagine what their future might look like. But today kids and grandkids grow up many miles and states away from aging relatives. It's hard to picture the future so it's hard to build a good roadmap to the future. And if we can't keep our eyes on the goal we are toast.

And the younger we are, the further the goal line, the longer the marathon, and the "toastier" we'll be.

When we picture ourselves in the future, what do we picture ourselves doing? And remember, we can only do nothing for so long before we die from boredom. What do you like to do in your free time now? What things do you do now that are most life-giving?

It is helpful for us to picture what our future will look like, what we might even look like, in 20 or 30 or 40 years or maybe it's helpful to first define what we do not want our future to be (like moving in with Jr.).

I had a retirement plan participant tell me once "I'm just gonna move in with my son." She was trying to be funny, but she was kind of serious too. It was sad because she was young enough that it did not have to be her only option. She had already resigned herself to not finishing the race or reaching the goal line and she was barely at the 50-yard line.

My first thought was, "I wonder what your son thinks about that."

My second thought was, "I wonder what your daughter-in-law will think about that plan."

They may not be quite as thrilled with the idea and they probably won't think it's quite as funny as she did in the employee meeting that day. She was trying to be funny, but I thought she was being selfish. Being a burden on our kids should not be our retirement plan. After all, children should not have to save up for their parents, but parents for their children.[1]

But then I had another thought, because there was something redeeming about her attempt at being funny. When she said it, I could see in the eyes of her co-workers the recognition of what they did not want their retirement goal to be. I imagine they were thinking, "That will not be me; my retirement dream is not to be a burden on my kids."

I'm still sad for her but I believe others in the room that day might retire better because they were given a glimpse of what they did not want their retirement goal to be. It was like a visit from the ghost of Christmas future, and it changed their behavior.

Many Americans could probably benefit from a similar wakeup call. Did you know 14 ½ percent of Americans live below the poverty level?[2] Many who are within the group are at or beyond age 65. Generally speaking, many of us are not finishing the race well. It's more like we are limping across the finish line, struggling to not outlive our money.

Part of the issue is what I call the **tangibility gap**, the gap between our certain present and our intangible future. If the future is hard for us to visualize and imagine it's more akin to science fiction than the indicators needed for a reliable roadmap.

Shlomo Bernartzi, a thought leader in the world of Behavioral Finance, suggests we need to have a computer program which will allow employees to see an age progression of their face when making decisions about how much to invest for the future.

In our firm we use an app when meeting with employees (yes, there's an app for that too).[3] It allows us to take a picture of the employee, enter their current age, then age-progress the photo to a future date right in front of them. We think it helps, that higher participation rates and higher savings rates are the fruit of employees taking the future more seriously.

Perhaps in the company retirement plan meetings of the future we will use time machines to show employees potential outcomes of investing or not investing, a glimpse decades into the future to bridge the tangibility gap. Of course, counselors would need to be on hand in case the future picture of themselves did not include the same spouse with whom they stepped into the time machine at the meeting. But it would solve for an intangible future.

Another part of the issue is what psychologists refer to as the Pygmalion effect. It says people live up to or down to the expectations others have of them.

Often evidenced in the classroom, I have seen this played out in soccer many times with my son's team. One of his friends on an early squad was a bit of an underachiever. He changed teams and several years later we saw him on the field again as a completely different player. Remembering the kid who was always screwing around, another parent said, "Can you believe that's so-and-so out there?" as if it was beyond comprehension. My thought was how sad we would ever give up on a kid. We play up (or down) to expectations.

Aware of this phenomenon, I try to picture every plan participant like my dad, really smart and fully capable of finishing the race well if they just have the right encouragement from someone who believes in them.

The Pygmalion effect works on ourselves with expectations too. If we can't picture ourselves crossing the goal line, we'll trip. We will be our own worst enemy.

MISTAKE # 2 – NOT USING TODAY TO FUND TOMORROW

Behavioral Finance teaches that another hindrance to sound decision making is what we call the **present bias**,[4] the tendency to overweight the present at the expense of long-term rewards in the future, to focus on what we have or don't have today rather than on what we need for tomorrow.

Some have described retirement as a kind of vacation, albeit a really, really long vacation. It's not a great definition but it's not a bad starting point since we have all taken a vacation while fewer of us have taken retirement. So imagining retirement as a type of extended vacation might help bridge the Tangibility Gap.

Vacations are designed as a sabbatical, a respite or short-term relief from the unpleasantries, a break from life, doing what we'd like to do. But imagine getting kind of used to doing whatever we want to do, whether it's fishing all day or writing the next great American novel or doing absolutely nothing. After two weeks of doing nothing it might even become a habit. And imagine we were having so much cotton-pickin' fun[5] we call the boss and say, "I'd like to extend this little vacation I'm on for another month…or two…or maybe a few years…maybe even 20 or 30 years."

That is kind of what retirement is: a 20- or 30- or 40-year vacation. Longer for some, depending on life expectancy. It's a really long break. If we take a vacation from work our employer pays. But who is responsible for paying for the 20- or 30-year vacation?

This is where the analogy falls apart. There are two major issues with picturing retirement as a decades long vacation. For starters, how does one pay for such a long vacation, not working for nearly as long as we did work? If the typical person starts working at 25 and works until age 65, they collect a paycheck for four decades. Life expectancy today is well into the 80's but most of us know someone in their 90's and centenarians are the fastest growing segment of our population. In fact, according to the Office for National Statistics in the UK, one-third of babies born in 2013 are expected to live to 100.[6]

How does the math work on collecting a paycheck 40 years and then not collecting a paycheck the next 40 years? Is it complicated math?

One option could be to live on only half of what we make in the first 40 years, stuffing the other 50% under the mattress, and live on the other half during the next 40 years.

Let's call it the 50/50 plan.

Case solved!

THE END

Everyone flips the page on that option because while it is one option it is not a very reasonable option. Setting the 401(k) contribution at 50% is completely unreasonable.

Fortunately, most people will not need as much in the second 40 years as they did in the first 40 years, so not only is the 50/50 plan not palatable it's not even necessary.

What if during the first 40 years a person pays for and pays off all the really big purchases, like college and home, so when they retire, they have ZERO DEBT? Few working Americans are debt free, but all retirees had better be debt free ... it's the only way the math works. Plus, it allows us to move from the 50/50 plan to the 70/30 plan (living on 70% in the first half of life and living on the other 30% in the second half).

Or what if, rather than just sticking 30% in a bank account or under the mattress or in an annuity, a person could earn money on their money? Maybe a person could get away with saving only 15% if they invested well, and if they started saving 15% early.

The 85/15 plan works much better, and the math works too.

Some will complain about the idea of living on only 85% of what they make, but the alternative is much less reasonable (living on only 50%). Imagine the beauty of living on as **much** as 85% and then getting away with funding a decades long vacation with only 15%.

This is amazing! It's not some kind of voodoo economics, and it's not science fiction, and it's not a pipe dream. It is reality – or it can be – for every American. And I'm not talking about living on 85% now and 15% later as a reduction in lifestyle. I am suggesting replacing our current lifestyle in retirement, that the lifestyle which now requires 85% of our income should only take 15% of current income to fund in retirement.

MISTAKE # 3 – THINKING RETIREMENT IS THE GOAL

The analogy of retirement as a vacation falls short. There are at least two major issues with picturing retirement as a decades long vacation. The first was cost, but the second major issue is an even bigger obstacle. It has to do with purpose. After all, is any vacation worth doing for decades? Doing nothing for a few weeks sounds nice but doing nothing for years on end sounds boring at best and purposeless at worst.

For that reason, the goal is not retirement.

The goal of a retirement savings account is not just retirement. The 401(k) is a tool, an investment vehicle, used to build wealth and gain financial freedom to do whatever we are called to do as soon as we know what it is and can afford to pursue it. We must move beyond this antiquated notion of checking out and doing nothing, like putting a horse out to pasture.

We also must get beyond the idea that retirement is an age. When they started saying retirement was age 65[7], people did not generally live much beyond 65, but today life expectancy is longer.

Studies have shown that on average, Americans who retire earlier often do not live as long. When they lost their career, they lost the opportunity for productivity which provided a great deal more than just a paycheck; the job had lent a great deal more to quality of life and overall happiness than many realize. They didn't just lose a job that paid the bills but a source of purpose and esteem that paid dividends in significance and satisfaction. A vacation does not do that. A vacation is a nice respite or sabbatical for a period of time, but it is not how we want to spend decades on this planet.

As previously stated, according to a USA Today survey, the number-one activity of Americans over age 65 is watching television.[8] Which makes particularly interesting the study cited by Paul Dolan in "Happiness by Design." According to Dr. Dolan, very few people found more pleasure than purpose in their work and very few found more purpose than pleasure in watching TV. That gets at the heart of this balancing act between pleasure and purpose. Happiness has for too long been thought of as simply a pursuit of pleasure but it has to be a balance between pleasure and purpose. The problem with the movement into retirement from a working career in which we had any degree of purpose is we are trading one primary activity (work) which gives us purpose for another primary activity (watching TV) which only gives us pleasure.[9]

Feel free to substitute other leisure activities, like playing golf, but the point remains: meaningful work provides purpose, purpose from which we might not want to completely take a vacation. The analogy of a vacation might help bridge the tangibility gap but it falls short because even the greatest vacation in the world (the trip of a lifetime; the African safari; the cruise to the Bahamas; traveling to Maui or Tahiti or Rome or Yee Haw Junction; hiking the Himalayas or the Grand Tetons or the Appalachian Trail) is not worth forty years of your life in preparation.

Retirement, to have purpose, has to mean something more than just getting away for a while.

And yet the word "retire" comes from an old French word "retirer" meaning "to withdraw" or "to retreat." Originally the context was military as in "to withdraw from one's position" or "to recede." Somehow it also became appropriate to describe someone who was "going to bed" and then eventually someone who would no longer work for a living.

It had better be an incredible sleep to be worthy of 40 years of your life!

Or if they are not sleeping, retirees spend an inordinate amount of time watching TV. Maybe part of why we have a retirement crisis in America is because our vision of retirement is about as inspiring as a remote control and a La-Z-Boy recliner. The average American takes fewer vacations than the average European, working harder as if we are racing towards a finish line, only to arrive and learn our big prize is watching re-runs.

I suggest rather than retreat *from* the field of battle or *to* the TV we should be engaging the world. As we age, we accumulate a ton of life experiences and sharing it with the next generation benefits the giver and the recipient. I believe a more fitting term than retirement is "Repurposement."

What if this transition was more about following our dreams, perhaps beyond age 65, or perhaps much sooner if we are financially independent? The "retirement years" should be the most productive, fruitful, fulfilling years of our life, graduating from the job we had to have to the job we want to have. If a person can do it in their youth it is even better, but if it takes them until age 50 or 60 to have the financial resources to pursue, then perhaps they become an encore entrepreneur.

What's wrong with retirement in America? It's a much larger problem than the economics (yes, it's underfunded). The much bigger problem is retirement is seen as retreating, withdrawing, disengaging, checking out, giving up, to rest...or worse yet...to just to watch TV. Retirement should be Engaging not Disengaging.

What if we viewed the first half of our working years as the preparation or training or equipping for the second half? And what if our working years was simply laying the foundation for the legacy or mission we will devote our lives to?

And what if we viewed the "halftime" as "Repurposement," as if the second chapter or second half of our lives was the purpose for which we have been preparing all along?

I believe each person has a unique purpose, expressed in their calling, which is shaped by their gifts and talents, what they are passionate about and uniquely qualified to do. The calling is expressed in a job. The job is important because it pays the rent, but more so because it provides an outlet for their calling.

Your purpose is your WHO … who you are.

Your calling is your WHY … why you do what you do.

And then the job is your WHAT.

I remember hearing a pastor once share who we are is not what we do any more than what we do is who we are. Sounds simple enough, but if this is misunderstood then someone who loses their job tailspins into a kind of identify crisis. Others who retire from a job they thought defined their purpose face a meaningless retirement, floundering between boredom and depression. Your purpose, once you discover who you are, does not change. Your calling, your WHY can change a bit, shaped and defined as passions are discovered and defined over time. But our job changes all the time.[10]

Maybe our idea of retirement is upside down because our definition of purpose is upside down. If our purpose defines our calling which then defines our job, then the typical path does not make sense. The typical path is, after all, a downward spiral:

Work like a dog ... Retire ... Rest ... Death.

Meaningless, Meaningless. Everything is meaningless. What do people gain from all their labor?[11]

Meaningless labor can be used as a type of psychological warfare, which makes it all the more absurd that some employees voluntary engage in meaningless work.

A cruel example of harnessing meaningless labor to crush the human spirit was used by the Nazis to break the will of the prisoners in concentration camps, forcing them to dig endlessly day after day in a pointless manner devoid of any meaning. Each morning they were forced to dig, and towards the end of each day they were told to fill in the holes. The endless digging was difficult work, but it only became torturous when it became meaningless. Every morning the prisoners looked out at a field which looked the same as the previous day. No evidence of their work. Nothing to show for their efforts. No fruit for their labor.

Some retirees take up new hobbies like gardening, where the dirt (metaphorically and literally) does look different at the end of the day. But for some retirees who pass the day watching reruns it can look or at least feel a lot like digging up dirt only to fill it in again. Meaningless!

I think there is a better path, a purpose-driven path.

Rather than **working like a dog**, I would advocate for **finding your purpose**. It's about preparation and stewardship.

- Preparing for what? Watching TV for 40 years? No thanks! Take me out back and put me down.
- Stewarding what? Our time and resources to be FREE to pursue our purpose.

And rather than **retire**, I would advocate for **Repurposement**.

And rather than **rest**, I would rather pursue a **calling**, an engagement which is meaningful and life-giving. We rest to rejuvenate, recalibrate, replenish ... but what if our work was so fulfilling it was the source of rejuvenation and replenishment? That's a "calling," what each person is uniquely gifted and called to do. I'd like to think, just like George Bailey from *It's a Wonderful*

Life,[12] if we were given the gift of seeing what the world might look like if we had never been born, we would see a big fat hole only we could have filled. Find your passion and your work won't feel like labor from which you need to rest.

After all, rather than just settling for **death** our heart's desire is to aim for **legacy**, leaving something to this world greater than ourselves.

If the Typical Path is a descension –

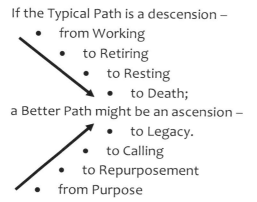

- from Working
  - to Retiring
    - to Resting
      - to Death;

a Better Path might be an ascension –

- to Legacy.
- to Calling
- to Repurposement
- from Purpose

Retirees who find significance in their job can be challenged by a post-career life of insignificance. Rather than preparation for the really important mission, the second phase of life is unfairly characterized as "downhill." What a shame it would be if we peak in significance halfway through the journey.

Let's say, for example, a person was elected President in our country at a very early age. Obama was 48 years old; Bill Clinton and Ulysses Grant were both 46; JFK was 43; but Teddy Roosevelt was the youngest at 42. Imagine reaching office at 42 (or even 35, the youngest possible age to be elected president). What JOB could one possibly hold after holding the presidency? What's next? I'm hoping, for their sanity and our benefit, their best work might still be in front of them, even if their last job was in the White House.

But for far too many of us, work equals significance, meaning "post-work" must equal post-significance.

Successful retirees (READ: happy and fulfilled), those who live with purpose and on purpose, those who find the golden years to truly be the richest and happiest years of their lives, know the key to really living is to leave a legacy, to give their **LIFE** away.

Labor,

Influence,

Finance and

Expertise.

Giving your LIFE away gives your life purpose, it gives retirees a reason for living, and it inspires the best in us because it puts the focus outside of us. Giving helps us focus on others.

Labor

Lucky indeed is the person who gets to work during the first half of their lives in a job which fits squarely with their passions. "Find the thing that you're passionate about and you'll never work a day in your life."[13]

However, most American workers change careers nearly as often as they changed their majors back in college. Once a person is ready to retire or repurpose they may have tried on dozens of careers to see which one fits best.

If we always wished we could volunteer more in the community, or at our church or synagogue, or supporting a particular cause or charity, we may have the chance to give our labor in that fashion. We could volunteer at the school or help raise grandkids or whatever we want to do now that we don't have to do something just for a paycheck.

Influence

Retirees can also use their influence to give back. They have amassed a wealth of life experiences and they could make a huge impact.

Influence is the power to change a person is said to be influential if they regularly change others or their environment in a significant way. Retirees should be among the most influential citizens in our country.

Or they can watch TV.

We're talking about the power to be a change agent, the power to make changes which change the world...

Or they can change channels with the remote.

FINANCE

In our country we are fond of describing (and not often in favorable terms) the "one percent" meaning those special privileged few who have amassed vast sums of wealth.

But if we were to line everybody up on this planet in order of net worth, there are few in America who would not be standing at the front of the line. From the world's perspective, Americans *are* the 1%. Those lucky enough to be born in this country were born with a wealth of opportunities.

Retirees should answer these two questions:

1) Who or what do they want to give their money to?

2) Who do they want their heirs to be?

Because there are no U-Hauls pulled behind those hearses.

We will either give the money to our heirs, to the charity or cause of our choice, or to the government. The IRS is my least favorite charity and I want to avoid that option. But I'm not stubborn enough to be buried with my treasure like an Egyptian prince. That just seems wasteful and selfish and silly.

Giving is a joy; giving during your lifetime allows you to experience the joy. Generosity is not measured by the number of zeros on the check but by the sincerity and purpose of the heart of the giver.[14]

EXPERTISE

There is no substitute for the wisdom gained from running the marathon, from years of creative problem solving and the accumulation of business acumen. There is no shortcut to experience. Even the most brilliant can't test their way out of it any more than the wealthy can buy their way into it. There is only one means of traversing this path, and it is through investing time.

Home associations need our expertise, as well as condo associations, or school boards, or church boards, or the board of our favorite charity. And business leaders have the opportunity to mentor young entrepreneurs.

Retirees who learn to give their **LIFE** away often learn giving it all away is the key to getting it all back again.[15] Realizing the goal is not retirement, but Repurposement; not disengagement, but re-engagement; not checking out but redeployment; for some they might discover the Golden Years to be the richest and most rewarding period of their life.

Retirement is not an age … it's a mindset.

Our goal should be financial independence, allowing us to be repurposed to pursue our calling as soon as we experience the intersection of our gifts and passions.

Understanding why people should want to build wealth is the key to making the 401(k) retirement vehicle work; it's the fuel to propel us towards a successful outcome. Before we can dig into a how-to book on how to make the 401(k) work, we need to understand our why.

1. 2 Corinthians 12:14, New International Version (NIV)
2. According to the U.S. Census Bureau statistics for 2013, the last available reporting year.
3. Face Retirement App from Merrill Edge®
4. O'Donoghue, T., & Rabin, M. (1999). Doing it now or later. *American Economic Review*, 89(1), 103-124.
5. That's something we used to say in Alabama. In the spirit of full disclosure, I have never picked cotton and it doesn't sound like it's that much fun.
6. ONS. 11 December 2013
7. Chancellor Otto von Bismarck of Germany used this age in the 1880's when introducing the new social security system, an age reached by hardly anyone in Germany at that time. Later the same age was used in 1935 when the US adopted what became Social Security in this country. But the age has remained at 65 despite advances in healthcare that now allow Americans to outlive this milestone by many decades.
8. The average American watches 5 hours of TV per day, but the average retiree spends more than 8 hours a day sitting in front of their televisions, approximately 50 hours a week, *NY Times*. 5 March 2014. And the numbers are increasing. In a 2009 study, "Television & Health" by California State University, Northridge, the average 65-year-old spent 9 years in front of the television (more than 4 h/day, 28 h/week). According to a July 8, 2013 US News & World Report article, "How Retirees Spend Their Time," retirees spend half of their newfound leisure time watching television. Two years later USA Today conducted a study which netted the same results, with an even larger number of hours spent watching TV.
9. Happiness by Design: Change what you do, not how you think, by Paul Dolan, PhD, Hudson Street Press, 2014.
10. Individuals born in the latter years of the baby boom (1957-1964) held an average of 11.9 jobs from age 18 to age 50, according to the U.S. Bureau of Labor Statistics, U.S. Department of Labor, News Release, August 24, 2017.
11. Ecclesiastes 1:2-3
12. It's a Wonderful Life, 1946 film.
13. Confucius is often attributed with the quote: "Choose a job you love, and you will never have to work a day in your life."
14. I would highly recommend the book "Giving it All Away … and Getting it all Back Again – The way of Living Generously" by David Green (Founder & CEO of Hobby Lobby) with Bill High. Zondervan. 2017.
15. ibid

CHAPTER 2
THE RULE OF 70
Retirement is not an age. It's a percentage.

A few years ago, an insurance company[1] crafted a campaign asking, "Do you know your number?" The commercials depicted neighbors talking about how much they needed to retire (their "number"). The numbers were huge, 7-8-digit figures which spoke to the enormous price tag for retirement. In each of the spots one person knew their number (presumably thanks to this insurance company) and the other person was clueless. The cluelessness invoked fear.

It was effective in raising awareness and momentarily scaring us into some productive dialogue. But, because the number was so daunting, the formula so specious, and the solution so ambiguous, it did not have a lasting effect on our decision making or behavior.

Some say a person needs a million dollars to retire these days. Others insist two million (or more) is the requirement. Missing in this discourse is the primary objective of retirement, which is income replacement, trying to replace current income to be repurposed later.

Saying a person needs a million dollars to retire is hogwash! It depends on how much a person makes, how much they owe, their current lifestyle and their projected lifestyle. It also depends on their calling, their purpose, and what they will be doing when they are repurposed or redeployed. It depends on a ton of factors.

A person does not need a million dollars to retire if they make $30,000 a year, and if they make $150,000 a year, a million may not be enough. Everyone's "number" is relative.

Retirement is not an age or a number; it's a percentage.

Repurposement is definitely not an age because a person can be repurposed at any time, as soon as they identify their purpose, see the occasion, and are financially able to seize the opportunity.

Aiming to invest as much as possible until "retirement age" is not the goal. After all, what if they accumulate "enough" prior to retirement age?

Aiming at an age places the locus of control outside of ourselves, bound by the day we happen to be born. Aiming at an amount is much more constructive and empowering for planning purposes.

If we over-fire we may be assuming more risk than necessary, not ensuring we hit the target. It's not like hunting with a shotgun and simply spewing as much firepower as possible 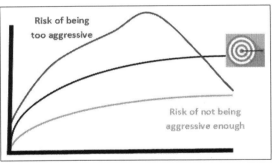 in a haphazard fashion, hoping to hit something. Nor is this exercise in target practice accomplished by sending a bazooka to do the job of a rifle. A person can shoot beyond the target which can be just as big of an error as the shot falling short.

Or a person could blow themselves up with being too aggressive and using too much firepower.

Americans have not taken their retirement investments seriously enough, and clearly most will not have enough. The looming question is why it is worth the effort to invest, why it is worth the discipline to make our money behave.

If the primary reason for wanting to retire is to stop working because we hate our jobs...we may simply need a different job, not retirement. I believe we were created to find joy in our labor, and if we are not finding joy, there is either something to fix in what we are laboring at or something to fix in us. Our aim should be financial independence, becoming the master of our domain rather than the victim of circumstances.

By no means am I a marksman or even knowledgeable in a pedestrian fashion about guns or archery, so this analogy may break down quickly. But it seems, in my uninitiated mind, in order to hit the target we are aiming at, it requires some calibration or knowledge of where we are and where we want to aim.

The target for Repurposement is income replacement. In other words, goal is to replace our income so we can stop working at the JOB we are not passionate about and get to do the hobby or calling we *are* passionate about.

In the investment world we understand there is a correlation between risk and reward. More risk merits higher rewards (i.e., higher investment returns). Otherwise, why expose a portfolio to unnecessary risk, if not for the opportunity for greater returns? But does greater and greater risk necessarily produce higher and higher returns?

Modern Portfolio Theory[2] teaches that in an efficient market greater risk produces greater rewards, to a certain extent, but beyond that point (the point of the "Efficient Frontier") the correlation breaks down. There should be an appropriate amount of risk to garner the desired amount of return. But there is also a point at which an investor is assuming more risk than necessary for the desired amount of return because beyond the Efficient Frontier the investor is assuming greater risk without experiencing commensurate reward.

The principal holds true for individual investments, but it also applies to the investment vehicles we know as 401(k) plans; with the overall portfolio there is an appropriate amount of risk to assume which yields the appropriate level of reward to hit the goal. Assuming more risk with individual securities may not yield more reward and may be inefficient; assuming more risk with the overall portfolio may not hit the target, and in certain market conditions may in fact fall short of the target, and may not be prudent.

Let's say, for instance, a person makes $60,000 a year. Presumably they are living on $60,000 if making $60,000. (Some people live under their means. Most live beyond their means. For this illustration, let's assume they are living within their means.)

The goal of Repurposement is to replace our current lifestyle, to replace our current income so we can stop collecting a paycheck from the JOB[3] and start paying ourselves.

"How much of your current income would you like to replace?"

Is it a trick question? Most would say 100%; few desire less than 100%.

But most everybody will live on less in retirement than they do during their working years.

During the first half of life, when they are in the accumulation phase, they are also paying off all of the really big ticket items (or should be), like the house and car and college, etc., so during the "Golden Years" they might presumably need less Gold to make ends meet.

Ironically a person should need less GOLD in their Golden Years.[4] Some people, if they have invested wisely, may have more, but most will need less. And there are essentially two ways to *"give ourselves a raise"*: increase income while maintaining the same financial obligations or reduce expenses and obligations.

With less need, income replacement of 90% or 80% or even 70% is enough. Most financial advisors suggest income replacement between 70% and 80%, both because it is sufficient but also because it is achievable. Parenthetically, if a financial adviser promises income replacement of 100% or more ... get a second opinion – it's unrealistic and unnecessary.

I recommend income replacement of 70%. It is an attainable goal, and everyone should all be able to replace 70% (or more) of their income.

To replace more is fine. I seldom hear a retiree complain, "Gee, I invested too much!"

But, replacing less is not fine. Replacing less than 70% of our income will almost certainly mean an adjustment in lifestyle. And I hear far too many retirees wish they had invested more when they were younger.

Another reason 70% works well is because Social Security replaces about a third of what the average retiree needs.[5] Admittedly, social security checks are not growing larger, but they still supplement our portion. If we replace 70% or more and expenses go down, social security provides some nice *icing on the cake.*

I call this **the Rule of 70**. It's *the ability to replace 70% or more* of income *and to live on 70% or less* of our income.

And that is the key. Some people have trouble living within their means (living on less than 100%) so the idea of living on 70% (or less) sounds impossible.

➢ Replacing 70% (or more) means being a good steward.
➢ Living on 70% (or less) means retiring debt free.
➢ Stewardship and debt free living are essential to success.

How can one ever replace 70% of their income? By living on less than they make and investing some of what they make now to fund the future. If they live on 85% and invest the rest, they have a good chance of successful Repurposement, perhaps earlier than the typical "retirement age."

But if they live on 100% of what they make they will not be successful.

And many Americas live on more than 100% of what they make using plastic rather than cash.

If folks can't learn to live within their means during the first half of their life, the chance of successfully navigating life when the income drops is daunting. The average American has 24% of their paycheck going towards consumer debt.[6]

Our enslavement to debt is the lifeblood of the credit card industry. And this notion that we must have a great credit score is part of the subterfuge designed to encourage more borrowing and greater enslavement. The FICO score might as well stand for "Foolish Incarceration to Consumer Obligations" because we are doing it to ourselves.[7]

A high FICO score might just mean "I love debt!" It is not part of learning to live within our means.

Everyone needs to learn to live within their means, which will periodically mean tightening the budget to say no. Dave Ramsey says, "I've got good news and bad news. The bad news is you're going to have to tighten your belt and reduce your spending, but the good news is you get to choose when."

We have two options: we can make some touch choices now, getting our money under control now, when it's our choice ... or we will *have to* later, when we don't have a choice.

One path might have a person living on nearly everything they make now with a huge reduction in lifestyle later. Another path might have a person living like a pauper now to fund a fabulous lifestyle later (which could work ... if we live long enough to enjoy the spoils of decades of sacrifice).

To me, the better path would be a manageable lifestyle now to fund a comfortable retirement later.

Retirement Challenge

A person can test whether they are on track for Repurposement by voluntarily choosing to live on 70% and asking whether their current investments could replace 70% of income. Someone who is within 3-6 months of repurposing can "try it on for size" to see how it fits by changing their contribution rate within the 401(k) plan to 30% before they step off the precipice into the next chapter.

The person who says, "You're insane! I could never live on only 70% of what I make!" ... may not be ready to take the step.

It is not uncommon for a 401(k) plan participant to say, "I'm barely making it now on 95% — investing 5% in the plan. I couldn't live on less than 95%." And yet very few Americans have invested enough to replace 95% or more of their income.

If a person is barely making ends meet on 95% of their income, they need to reduce their lifestyle or reduce their debt ... or both.

For some employees, this idea of practicing for Repurposement with the "Retirement Challenge" provides a great opportunity to see what life after separation from the company might look like.

For some it *can* be a blessing.

For most it is a wake-up call, which might still be a blessing if the wake-up call initiates behavioral changes that prompts a reduction in lifestyle. But the sad reality is far too many Americans don't get the wake-up call until it is too late in life.

Retirement is not an age but a percentage, the ability to replace 70% or more and the ability to live on 70% or less.

If a person can replace more, fantastic! And if they have so few obligations they can live on even less, even better. But shooting for 70 will get most of us on target for Repurposement.

Time, Myopia and Mr. Magoo

Time horizon is another key ingredient to consider for success. The earlier we start this journey, the more successful the outcome. How far along we are on the journey should impact our allocations and investment choices. And our perspective on the length of the marathon directly impacts our ability to complete the race. Unfortunately, our expectations can be off, our perspectives clouded by poor vision and short-sighted thinking.

In the 1950's, Quincy Magoo, known simply as Mr. Magoo, was a popular cartoon depicting the misadventures of an extremely myopic elderly gentleman who was constantly stepping into the disastrous consequences of short-sightedness.

The fictional Mr. Magoo is depicted as wealthy and retirement age; but generally, short-sightedness inhibits efforts to build wealth or retire well.

Magoo literally fell into a series of misfortunes due to his poor eyesight, compounded by his stubborn refusal to admit his visual impairment. The cartoon maintains a comic edge because none of Magoo's missteps actually lead to catastrophic or fatal conclusions, but anyone dealing with myopia knows this is anything but a laughing matter.

I was born extremely myopic. The "coke-bottle" glasses I wore vaulted me to a notoriety from which my self-esteem barely survived. By high school I had switched to contacts and as a young adult I had LASIK eye surgery.

Myopia or near-sightedness is a condition of the eye where the image forms in front of the retina because of the oblong, oversized length of the eyeball. In LASIK, as with glasses or contacts, the correction is to the lens, to refocus the image further back onto the retina. They fixed the lens in the "camera", but the shape of the eyeball was still oblong.

When I was only 39 years old, the retina in my right eye detached, pulling loose from the back of the oblong eyeball. They reattached it but it detached again, and after multiple surgeries the "film" in the "camera" doesn't work the same because of extreme myopia.

Behaviorally speaking, most people are myopic to some degree. This is true for decision-making and true of how we handle money. It is particularly true of how we prepare for retirement.

The word "Myopia" literally means "short-sighted" and a major tenant of Behavioral Finance is the short-sighted approach most of us have with money management. One example is what behavioral economists refer to as the "money illusion"[8] meaning our tendency to think of currency in nominal rather than real terms. In other words, the face value, or nominal value of what is printed on the face of the money is mistaken for the actual purchasing power.

(what the currency reads)		(Purchasing value or inflation)	(actual impact on wallet)		
Nominal Value		Monetary Value	Purchasing Power		Perception
$100	-2%	$98.00	0%	$98	Unfair
$100	2%	$102.00	-4%	$98	Fair

Another way short-sightedness can impact some of the decision-making is evidenced in what is called the Myopic Loss Aversion Theory.[9] Dr. Shlomo Benartzi et al. have demonstrated we are loss averse, that we feel losses twice as much as we feel gains. It impacts our perception of outcomes and distorts the image of the rational choice. Experiments have demonstrated, for example, we perceive a 2% cut in nominal income (the face value of money) with no change in monetary value (inflation) as unfair, but we see a 2% rise in nominal income when there is 4% inflation as fair. In both scenarios, there is a loss in "purchasing power" of exactly 2% but myopic thinking keeps us from seeing these as rational equivalents.

I find this fascinating because I see so many parallels between the physical affliction which has compromised my vision and the myopic affliction that is part of the human condition. In behavioral finance myopia is evidenced in the "Present Bias," the tendency to overly emphasize what is right in front of us without having a long-term perspective. Loss or pain today is perceived as much more unpleasant than future loss or future pain. Hyperbolic discounting suggests we would prefer a dollar today to $3 in one year, for example. The bottom line is when time is involved, money decisions are distorted. But decision-making is often skewed through the prism of time. In my first career, I tried to help people understand the impact of each day on tomorrow, how decisions and actions today could affect their future. In my second career, the conversations are not dissimilar because myopia distorts the future impact of current decisions.

For example, few people would intend to spend $602,553.09 on a car, but because of myopic, short-term thinking, this is effectively what happens.

- A $20,000 vehicle could be purchased in cash for $20,000
- Or it could be paid in monthly payments of $500 for 5 years.
- $500 a month or $6,000 a year equals $30,000 over 5 years.
- We accept the additional cost of interest without calculating the real cost.
- Investing $500 a month for 60 months in the 401(k) plan at a modest 8% rate of return nets $602,553.09 at retirement.

If we do the math we do not feel great about spending $30,000 for the car priced at $20,000 but if we did the real math and calculated the loss of purchasing power, the power of what $30,000 invested could have purchased, it might make us too sick to drive the car.

As Richard Thaler points out, "All economic decisions are made through the lens of opportunity costs."[10]

Webster's Dictionary defines myopia as the ophthalmologic condition of nearsightedness which compromised my vision. But Webster's also offers a secondary definition: "the lack of foresight or discernment; obtuseness" and that is the condition which is impacting retirement in America today.

The good news is behavioral finance not only identifies behavioral challenges but also offers behavioral solutions (generally through plan design). For instance, because we know most people overemphasize the now as compared to some future period, redesigning the choice architecture to solve for short-term thinking makes the economic decisions nearly "dummy proof." The tendency to overvalue the immediate (also called the "immediacy effect") means people generally care much more about their present selves than their future selves, which relates to a variety of arenas, from weight loss and addiction recovery to economic decisions.

In retirement we have the compounded effect of an incredibly long-time horizon plus the difficulty relating to our future selves (the "Tangibility Gap"). In fact, an experiment demonstrated our preference or appreciation for our future selves is no greater than for that of a complete stranger, and putting money into the 401(k) can be felt (by some) like giving money to someone we don't even know.

The experiment tested the emotional impulses (measuring cognitive data through electrical impulses) of what a person experiences when they give away money. (The response was pain, not pleasure.) Giving money to a stranger, according to the pain centers of the brain, is very unpleasant. On the other hand, the emotional response of giving it to someone we know and like is much more pleasant.

But when test subjects were shown an age-progressed picture of themselves and asked to give money to their future self it was discovered we feel only slightly less pain in giving it to our future self than to a complete stranger.

The challenge for retirement plan design is to help us make future decisions with a positive long-term impact on outcomes. When asked if we would invest 10% today or 10% in a few years, most of us choose to invest more if it is a future decision (like deferring the pain and the deferral). This is the science behind automatic increases in contributions. The auto-features in 401(k) plans are in place to overcome our short-sightedness.

- Knowing our tendency to be myopic in money matters, if our company offers a 401(k) plan, we should allow ourselves to be automatically enrolled and allow our contribution rate to be automatically nudged[11] each year until we get to the appropriate investment rate.
- If we do not have a 401k available (or 403b or 457 plan) we should open an IRA. But do not make it dependent on the monthly discipline send the check; have it automatically debited.
- And use the "auto-diversification" option, the default investment, to diversify and automatically rebalance the portfolio. The appropriate diversification must not be dependent on our ability to time the market or rebalance it ourselves. Just automate it.

A 401(k) contribution is a type of commitment strategy (pre-committing ourselves in advance to invest with each pay period). After all, the contributions work because payroll doesn't ask each week if we still want to invest the money for that check; the contributions are made automatically. A decision (at enrollment or at the beginning of the plan year) benefits us all year long.

Auto features just take it one step further. They are future decisions made now which will positively impact our account later. It solves for our human tendency to make the wrong current decision by making future choices today.

Webster's also defines "Myopic" as "unable or unwilling to act prudently; shortsighted" which summarizes the fundamental issue with retirement today.

The trouble with ERISA's **Prudent Man Rule**, is the the Prudent Man is confounded by the Myopic Man, who is unable or unwilling to act or see the way to act prudently.

1. At the time of these commercials, the insurance company was known as ING (International Netherlands Group), a Dutch multinational banking company. The company has since rebranded itself as Voya, the American financial services company which operates as a subsidiary of ING Group.

2. A systematic approach of maximizing returns for a particular level of risk, first introduced in a 1952 essay from economist Harry Markowitz for which he later won the Nobel Prize in Economics.

3. Throughout this book, "job" is used almost universally as a pejorative term. When speaking favorably about a person's means of employment, another descriptive will be used.

4. In "Ready! Fire! Aim? 2018," J.P. Morgan Asset Management reported spending increases right before retirement, peaking at retirement and decreasing thereafter. The evidence of spending surging at retirement was based on Chase credit card, debit card, electronic payments, ATM withdrawals, and check transactions with other bank customers and information that would have allowed identification of specific customers was removed prior to the analysis. The conclusion was it takes money to retire, and some spend more in retirement than they did during the accumulation phase, but most Americans spend the most right before retirement and then significantly less after retirement.

5. Income replacement is about one-third on average but varies widely depending on household income. According to the "Guide to Retirement," 2019 Edition, p. 16, a household earning $30k has 60% of income replacement from Social Security, a household earning $100k has 38%, a household earning $300k has 12%.

6. U.S. Census Bureau, 2014.

7. FICO actually stands for Fair, Isaac, and Company, because Bill Fair and Earl Isaacs developed the rating system in the 1950's to gauge the risk of lending money based upon the likelihood of a borrower's repayment. They developed FICO scores, and like lambs to the slaughter we foolishly rushed out to increase our FICO scores. A higher FICO score simply indicates more money borrowed and repaid.

8. Money illusion is an economic theory stating many people have a false picture of their wealth based on nominal dollar terms rather than real terms. The term was coined by Irving Fisher in *Stabilizing the Dollar*. It was popularized by John Maynard Keynes in the early twentieth century, and Irving Fisher wrote an important book on the subject, *The Money Illusion*, in 1928. Differentiated from nominal dollar terms, the actual cost takes into account the level of inflation in an economy.

9. Myopic loss aversion occurs when investors take a view of their investments that is strongly focused on the short term, leading them to react too negatively to recent losses, which may be at the expense of long-term benefits (Richard Thaler et al., 1997).

10. "Misbehaving: The Making of Behavioral Economics," Richard Thaler, 2015. P. 57.

11. This is a reference to "Nudge: Improving Decisions about Health, Wealth and Happiness," by Richard Thaler and Cass Sunstein, Yale University Press, April, 2008.

CHAPTER 3
THE FREEDOM OF BUDGETING
Creating the roadmap to success with money.

There was a time in the not too distant past, prior to guidance from Garmin or Siri, when paper maps were the only alternative, when navigational prowess was evidenced by the deft skills of unfolding and re-folding large sections of printed directions, only to discover the desired destination inevitably fell on a worn or torn seam of the fold. With the transition to a digital world we lost the value of a roadmap on paper just as we lost the value of putting pen to paper.

The point is there is something psychologically and functionally engendering to our confidence in drafting a roadmap and holding the document.

Many years ago, I was staying at a monastery in Cuernavaca, just south of Mexico City. One day I decided to take a walk-about and explore the village surrounding our compound, alone, without a phone (for calls or navigational purposes) and with a limited vocabulary in Spanish.

I was not carrying a map, but the monastery was on an elevated hill I reasoned could be seen from anywhere down the hill in the village. I made the mental note that the main street down into the village was named "Calle...something," and armed with renewed confidence I proceeded on my hike.

But after several hours, when I began to retrace my steps, the process proved to be quite difficult. I could not see the elevated buildings of the monastery from inside the village and most of the streets in Cuernavaca begin with Calle.[1]

I became anxious and my heart rate increased, and my decision-making was hindered as my confidence waned.

It took forever to find my way back and safely within the confines of the monastery I never ventured out again. My fear held me captive because I lacked the confidence to explore without a roadmap.

A written plan creates and builds confidence and greater confidence means we are more likely to act as the rational or "prudent man" would act; we make better decisions and we are less vulnerable to impulsive, poor decisions.

Having a written plan on paper will create greater financial peace.

Retirement plan participants do not need to be investment experts, but they need to be confident of what they know and confident in what they do not know (in what they need assistance with) so their money decisions are marked with wisdom.

Parenthetically, there is an important principal in psychology which impacts decision-making called the Dunning-Kruger Effect.[2] It is discussed further in the subsequent chapters on investments, but a brief description is the adverse relationship between those who need help and their willingness to ask for help. Those who venture far outside their expertise understand the need for assistance (as those in the financial industry might understand the need to hire an electrician, for example), but those barely acquainted with something may overestimate their proficiency, making them less likely to ask for advice. (A great example is someone whose only investment experience is their company 401k, and yet they shun the investment advice of their plan offers.) Conversely, the more someone knows about a particular subject the more likely they are to realize how much they do not know and the more likely they are to ask for help. Put bluntly, smart people ask for help, really smart people seek advice.

A hallmark of low ability or low understanding is unfortunately overconfidence leading to greater self-reliance (and greater errors in decision-making).

A written plan provides a general roadmap and informed investors would never embark on this journey without the map provided by a budget.

The first part of the Rule of 70 is built on the principal of stewardship, which is "managing our resources." To manage them we need to audit them, take assessment of them, and write them down.

We should write down a list of our debts, our obligations, our expenses, our income, and then figure out how we'll divide each dollar to make the money coming in match the needs of the money going out. (Remove credit cards as an option to fill the gap.) The total in Column A (money in) should zero out to the total in Column B (money out) because this is a zero-sum budget. A zero-sum budget "zeroes out" rather than going negative or positive. (Positive may sound good, but a positive budget means there is more coming in than going out and needs increased investments to zero out the budget, investing the surplus.)

How much to allocate towards a Rainy Day? Towards Savings? Towards Investing? Those are three completely different line items in the budget.

How much to allocate towards 'needs' (house, car, food and clothing) and 'wants' (like entertainment). And how much to allocate towards paying off debt. A person up to their eyeballs in debt must eliminate wants to eliminate debt.

The bottom line is everyone needs a budget:
> On paper
> On purpose
> On plan
> On budget

A budget needs to be on paper, on purpose, on plan, every month, without ceasing. Some will resist it initially, believing it's like wearing a straitjacket. But we are not restricting ourselves, we are restricting our money. We are taking control and telling it what to do. In effect, we are training our money to behave.

Training money to behave is not complicated, but retraining ourselves to handle money is hard. Part of the retraining is reminding ourselves we are in control. Our money works for us, not us for it. Except, of course, when we allow creditors to be in control because we are enslaved to debt.

Step one to taking back control: Keep it simple

The first step in taking control is to re-familiarize ourselves with money, with the feel of cold, hard cash. The quickest way to gain control of finances when one is completely out of control is to use a cash-only system. It awakens our sensitivities.

Behavioral Finance teaches that people are loss averse, that we feel a loss of money twice as much as we feel the gain of money, and we feel the loss much more if handing someone cash than handing them plastic.

Plastic money is fake money. It alleviates the pain of losing it.

The experts know less pain is triggered by the use of credit, if only because we are deferring the payment a bit. Studies show we spend more when using plastic. It's a basic tenant in the effort to separate us from our money.

Sometimes the plan to separate us from our money can work to our advantage but more often it is not in our best interest. The best example of plan design that is advantageous for us is in the 401(k) plan. The money goes into the 401(k) before we feel it or have a chance to spend it, so we never feel the loss of it. We are separated from our money for our own good. If it were up to us to send in the contribution each pay period, we might never do it.

But the perfect example of plan design employed to separate us from our money in a manner that disadvantages us is credit cards. And we use them promiscuously and spend beyond our zero-sum budget, trying to increase our FICO score and raise credit limits to color even further outside the lines.

We have lost touch with cash, we are numb to it, almost like we have been anesthetized. And just as people say and do stupid things when under anesthesia, we do dumb stuff with money when using plastic.

Using actual dollar bills puts us back in touch with the separation anxiety and pain. It may not be reasonable or safe to have a big pile of cash sitting around, but at least start with cash. Get an envelope (or jar) for each category in the budget and put actual cash in each envelope to control spending, only moving to an electronic version of this when the habit of staying on budget is deeply ingrained.[3]

At one point, speaking of a big pile of cash, it was rumored that the parent company of Google, Alphabet, had more cash reserves than any company in the world.[4] But they did not have so much cash that they could ignore the need to have a budget. And their budget actually has to balance, just like ours should. Google is the perfect example of a very important principle with budgeting: no one outlives, out-earns or outgrows the need to be on a budget. People who have a lot of money just have a bigger budget with more things to budget. But they (should) still have a budget. With fewer resources the margins for error are smaller, but with more resources comes more responsibility and the need to be even more proficient in training our money.

More cash might allow for a bigger margin of error but does not allow for skipping the budget. In fact, more money means more responsibility for stewardship. Seneca[5] said, "For many men, the acquisition of wealth does not end their troubles, it only changes them." I would say it complicates them. More is not the answer. "It is not the man who has too little," says Seneca, "but the man who craves more, that is poor."

So, the first step in getting on track with money is to use cash. If we must hand cash to the cashier, we think twice about whether the purchase is necessary.

The second step to getting on track with money is to do an audit of our spending, taking a month or two to write everything down. It will probably surprise us. And then, after assessing where the money went last month, make decisions about where it should go next month, which is the essence of a budget.

The Cup = Needs

A helpful analogy is to think of a budget as a series of cups. Certain essential cups that constitute needs are filled first. As these cups are filled the overflow runs onto the saucer below the cup which constitutes financial wellness. And below the saucer is a plate which constitutes the wants. The hope is to have the cup runneth over[6], with the overflow eventually filling all of the "buckets" in the budget. But the key is to get them in the right order.

The cup covers basic needs like food, shelter, clothing, and transportation, all of which involve some important choices to be made. A person may want to eat out, buy a bigger house, buy name brand clothing, and buy a new car, but they may need to eat at home, rent, buy affordable clothing, and buy a used car to make sure there is enough overflow to the cups below. A good cash-flow system allows cash to flow from needs to wants ... and does not confuse wants for needs. It starts with what is absolutely necessary, and then builds from there.

Seneca was once asked what the proper limit to wealth is. He said, "It is, first, to have what is necessary, and, second, to have what is enough."

Rather like psychologist Abraham Maslow's hierarchy of needs, our most basic needs must be met before we become motivated to achieve higher level needs. The need for financial wellness, for instance, is critical to financial "self-actualization" or "transcendence," but people are unlikely to pursue financial wellness until certain physiological needs are met.[7]

The SAUCER = FINANCIAL WELLNESS

Overflow allows one to get ahead with increased savings, elimination of debt, even elimination of the mortgage, and increased funds put aside for emergencies ... but there has to be overflow to make this happen. Currently, 70% of Americans live paycheck to paycheck with no overflow.[8] Most assume it is an income issue, but in most cases, it is a stewardship issue. They are lost without any map to navigate their valuable money.

Writing down what goes in each cup (or in the saucer) constitutes the roadmap, drafting the roadmap in pencil and allowing the flexibility to change it keeps it from feeling like a straitjacket. Because if it feels like a straitjacket (restrictive and punitive) then it is not a real budget. A good budget should be an empowering tool for better efficiencies, just as married couples should use the budget as a tool for better communication rather than a weapon.

Financial wellness is where the transformation happens. The number one cause of stress in America today is financial stress.[9] Because of poor money choices many Americans are not financially healthy which impacts a slew of other issues in their life, prevents them from having any overflow, and keeps them from ever getting ahead. I know an insurance salesman who was paid a variable amount of commission on a quarterly basis, and at the beginning of every quarter he always talked about "getting healthy." What he meant by that was paying off the credit cards when things ran short at the end of the previous quarter, when he ran out of money and needed some plastic money to bridge the gap until the real money came in. He thought he had a "commission issue" or a "quarterly payment issue" … but it was a budgeting issue.

Financial wellness involves three components: A **RAINY-DAY FUND**, the **DEBT SNOWBALL**, and the **SUNSHINE FUND**. It involves eliminating debt and getting ahead, stopping the payment of interest to creditors and receiving interest on the money we put to work. It's about identifying and maximizing margin, creating overflow and building financial peace. It's intentional and purposeful work because it does not happen on accident. It requires sound weather forecasting.

The Rainy-Day Fund

Foundational to every sound budget is elimination of debt but starting with a Rainy-Day Fund keeps us from spinning right back into debt … or taking two steps forward and three steps back.

If a person does not have a Rainy-Day Fund…it won't rain…it will pour.

The amount of the Rainy-Day Fund may depend on a person's lifestyle and means. It should probably not be less than $500, but some will suggest $1,000.[10] I would recommend even more if possible, and over time more will be possible if there is overflow.

The Debt Snowball

Once the Rainy-Day Fund is funded, to stop the bleeding, then (and only then) debt can be addressed, to start the healing. The debt occurred because we went off budget, consuming more than we produced. It might have been a huge accident that landed us in the ditch, but more likely we just slowly veered off course.

In most cases it took time to accrue the debt and will require time to eliminate the debt. But the fastest and most effective method is to list them from the smallest debt to the biggest debt, regardless of interest rate, and pay them off sequentially from smallest to largest in what's called the "debt snowball."[11] From a behavioral perspective it works because we gain momentum, we see results early, and we stick with the process long enough to get out from under the mountain of debt.

Others will argue the correct method is to pay off the debt with the highest interest first. This could make financial sense, but it does not make behavioral sense. Most people are prone to get discouraged and give up on reducing debt for the same reasons they sometimes give up on reducing weight: we quite if we don't see results fast enough.

The Sunshine Fund

The third part of the Saucer is preparing for the sunny day, the future date of financial independence when it is possible to be retired, repurposed, and/or become an encore entrepreneur. The Sunshine Fund is quite literally the light at the end of the tunnel, the gold at the end of the rainbow, the wealth as a reward for all the hard work, and there is no better[12] way to accumulate gold and build wealth than through the company-sponsored retirement plan (the 401k plan).

One could argue that another key component is the employer-sponsored Health Savings Account.[13] It makes sense for employees to only put enough in the 401(k) plan to receive the employer match, and then (with any overflow) to max out the HSA plan, since it offers triple-tax savings,[14] and then (with any additional overflow) max out the 401(k) up to the allowable limits.[15] The HSA is part of a good financial wellness plan[16] but the foundation of the plan is the company-sponsored 401(k).

The 401(k) is superior to an IRA or even the employer-sponsored SIMPLE IRA. It is lower cost than the IRA,[17] higher deferral limits than either the IRA or SIMPLE IRA, plus it has the advantages of Roth contributions that SIMPLE IRAs do not have. The 401(k) is wealth building and investing made simple: contributions are made on behalf of the employee before they miss them or have a chance to spend them, and in many cases contributions are matched by the employer as well.

The employer match complicates the correct order of events in financial wellness: snowballs and then sunshine, or sunshine before snowballs? It depends on the weather.

Without an employer match the answer is simple: 100% focus on the debt snowball before building wealth for a sunny day. But with an employer match, it depends on the size of the debt. For illustration purposes, let's say the match is 50% of 5%, and there are three buckets of varying amounts of debt. If one of the buckets could be eliminated quickly, within a few months, contribute nothing to the 401(k) until the small bucket of debt is empty. If one of the buckets could take years to eliminate, however, it might not make economic sense to forgo years of the match until the bucket of debt is empty, so contribute only enough to get the match (in this illustration, 5%) ... but not a penny more until the debt is gone. A guaranteed return[18] of 50% is hard to pass up. Investing 5% is not nearly enough, but eventually, when all the debt is eliminated, the contribution rate can be increased. For now, only do enough to get the match.

Imagine if a person could invest 25% rather than just 5%.[19] It sounds crazy, but 24% of the average American's paycheck is going towards consumer debt payments like credit cards and auto loans.[20] If a quarter of the average paycheck was not going to creditors it would create significant overflow.

The PLATE = WANTS

The plate constitutes the wants, an overflow from the needs, and an overflow from the saucer of financial wellness. With the

Cup-Saucer-Plate approach, a person doesn't get lost or have the anxiety-filled experience of losing their bearings on the journey to building wealth. It is the roadmap of success, the roadmap to build confidence to finish well.

Cup, then saucer, then plate. And there should not be any extra overflow to run off the plate. In a zero-sum budget, it all flows somewhere and "zeroes out." If there is extra, increase the allocations on the saucer towards getting ahead. Perhaps even increase the allocations towards the fun bucket on the plate.

Cup ⇨ Saucer ⇨ Plate: – it must be done in this order and eliminating any steps will make success much more difficult.

CUP-SAUCER-PLATE = ENOUGH

First the cup of needs. No one eliminates this element, of course, but some people put wants higher than needs.

Then the saucer of financial wellness. Eliminate this and we will have the situation of most Americans with needs and wants (or worse yet, wants and then needs) but never getting ahead. No financial cushion, tons of financial stress, crushing debt, and little investments. Without the saucer people fall into the trap of thinking their money issues are solved with more income. But when people make $1 more an hour, they find a way to spend $1 more an hour. In fact, hedonic adaptation[21] says that as we make more, we just raise our expectations.

When I was young, I struggled very little with discontentment (relative to what I later struggled with as an adult, not relative to other kids). It seemed like I had enough of whatever I needed. I was not aware of how little we had. There was food on the table, I had new clothes to wear each school year, there were gifts under the tree, and we always took a summer vacation. But we were lower-middle class. I never went to bed hungry, but my clothes were only new to me. And only later did I learn how my parents went into debt every Christmas to put gifts under the tree. And very few vacations did not involve destinations that allowed us to stay with family for free. It is a sad day indeed when the blindfold falls from our eyes and we realize we are not wearing the cool sneakers. The blissful innocence and financial ignorance of early childhood is shattered. And once a child catches a glimpse of their family's economic position, it cannot be unseen.

Enough has less to do with what we have and more to do with what we do not have. There will always be someone who has more toys. And thanks to hedonic adaptation, more toys does not mean more joy.

And then the plate of wants. Some people put the plate on top, which obviously does not work. Others put the plate below the cup and saucer, but they fill the plate, even going back for seconds, without any overflow. The plate is filled on credit.

Some people blame their circumstances or the size of their paycheck, and therefore they never get ahead financially. In some situations, the paycheck or job needs to change, but more often the problem is an outflow issue rather than an inflow issue, a budgeting issue rather than an income issue. The issue of having enough is an overflow issue, when the cup overflows.[22]

Building a roadmap is the key to winding up at the right destination, the secret to getting the currency correctly aligned so it flows in the right direction and overflows appropriately.

And the roadmap to building wealth and building the financial independence for Repurposement is a budget. It's basic 'mental accounting,' used to help with self-control, by predetermining buckets (physical buckets made of envelopes and mason jars, or electronic buckets like Mvelopes, to replicate mental buckets). Money is fungible, of course, but establishing a budget provides lanes for the currency to flow (and hopefully overflow).[23]

1. This has less to do with my grasp of Spanish and more to do with how decision-making under stress is compromised. I simply forgot that calle means street and that many roads in Cuernavaca have a name that starts with calle, especially those surrounding the Monasterio Benedictino, hence they all started to look and sound the same. I panicked.
2. In the field of psychology, the Dunning–Kruger effect is a cognitive bias in which people mistakenly assess their cognitive ability as greater than it is, first suggested in 2011 by social psychologists David Dunning and Justin Kruger.
3. Maintaining a cash-only system is not always practical, though it is the most practical way to start. Eventually move to a program that simulates a cash-only system. One option for envelope budgeting is a program called Mvelopes (Mvelopes.com) by Finicity.
4. We made no efforts to verify this. The point of the illustration is that whichever company has the most money still has a budget.
5. Seneca the Younger (c. 4 BC – AD 65), also known simply as Seneca, was a Roman Stoic philosopher.
6. Psalm 23.5
7. Maslow's hierarchy of needs is a theory in psychology proposed by Abraham Maslow in his 1943 paper "A Theory of Human Motivation."
8. According to a CNN Money 2013 survey.
9. According to the American Psychological Association.
10. Market Watch conducted a survey in 2015 that found 64% of Americans could not handle an emergency of even $1,000. So, having an extra thousand seems like a good idea to prepare for any speedbumps.
11. The debt-snowball method is a debt reduction strategy, whereby one who owes on more than one account pays off the accounts starting with the smallest balances first, while paying the minimum payment on larger debts, in contrast to the debt stacking method, also called the "debt avalanche method", where one pays off accounts on the highest interest rate first. The primary benefit of the smallest-balance plan is the psychological benefit of seeing results sooner. In a 2012 study by Northwestern's Kellogg School of Management, researchers found that consumers who tackle small balances first are likelier to eliminate their overall debt than trying to pay off high interest rate balances first. A 2016 study in Harvard Business Review came to a similar conclusion. ("Research: The Best Strategy for Paying Off Credit Card Debt". Harvard Business Review. 2017-03-17).
12. Better in the sense of consistent and proven methodology, excluding inconsistent methods of building wealth like gambling or winning the lottery, or even real estate, which can be a bit of a gamble in dealing with illiquid assets.
13. The HSA is only available if the employer offers a high-deductible medical plan.
14. The money goes in tax-free, grows tax-free, and comes out tax-free, if used for qualified medical expenses.
15. The maximum contribution limit is a dollar amount set each year by the IRS.
16. Not part of the medical benefits, as is often misunderstood, but part of the financial benefits, since it is an important tool in controlling spending and managing taxes. The use towards medical expenses cause some, even within the benefits industry, to mischaracterize this employee benefit as part of the health care and not wealth care.
17. Generally, an Individual Retirement Account (IRA) contains retail share class investments, while an institutional retirement account (like a 401k) contains institutional or retirement share class investments.
18. Not guaranteed in the sense of insurance annuities, but guaranteed by plan design, the employer's obligation to match the first 5% contributed.
19. Deferral limits set by the IRS may not allow everyone to contribute this much.
20. According to the US Census Bureau (2014).
21. The hedonic treadmill, also known as hedonic adaptation, is the observed tendency of people to quickly return to a relatively stable level of happiness despite major positive or negative events or life changes. Brickman and Campbell coined the term in their essay "Hedonic Relativism and Planning the Good Society" (1971).
22. Psalm 23.5
23. In economics, things of value are often interchangeable, so a dollar meant for one thing could be spent on another item or easily replaced.

CHAPTER 4
HOW MUCH?

The most important factor in building wealth.

There are two questions a person needs to answer to build wealth towards financial independence that allows for Repurposement. Just two things we have to know to make the 401(k) work. and one of them is markedly more important than the other.

The first question is HOW MUCH – as in *how much should a person invest for retirement?*

The second is WHERE – as in *where inside the 401k should they invest the money?*

Let's talk about HOW MUCH, and the evilness of averages.

This isn't how much do I *have* to invest, as in *how little can I get away with saving.* We want to avoid the evilness of averages and launch a successful path to Repurposement, not take the shortcut and wind up short of our goal. The simple answer to the question of how much fuel we should put in the tank is that it depends on how far we want to go.

It is helpful to know that HOW MUCH is much more important than WHERE. How much a person invests for retirement makes all the difference. Most people[1] assume that WHERE has a bigger impact, as if there is a magical mix of investments which captures the elusive goal of doubling their money overnight. But there are no shortcuts. It all depends on how much fuel is in the tank. The retirement vehicle has little chance of making the journey without enough gas.

Several independent studies confirmed the various success factors that produce healthy outcomes for employees in retirement plans. However, the conclusions and analysis of The American Society of Pension Professionals & Actuaries (ASPPA) codified the research in a fashion that changed belief systems within the industry.[2] The research found the least important driver of retirement success is the actual selection of the individual investment fund, what ASPPA termed the "asset quality." In other words, when choosing a particular investment (like which Large Cap Growth Fund or which Small Cap Value Fund to offer in the plan) the decision has very little impact on the long-term outcomes. The investment decision is not unimportant ... but it only drives 2% of the factor towards success.

According to ASPPA, the diversification of the investments (what ASPPA termed the "asset allocation") is ten times more important. In other words, it is less important which investment fund is chosen and more important the allocation of each employee towards each particular fund. If the trustees of the plan chose the XYZ fund over the ABC fund, it makes 2% of the difference, but whether an employee allocates 5% or 15% or 25% towards the XYZ fund makes 20% of the difference.

In terms of the "drivers of retirement success," the choice of which investment fund to offer (typically a decision made by the employer) and the choice of how to diversify investments within those funds offered (typically a decision made by the employee) accounts for 22% of the overall impact on retirement outcomes. The "asset quality" (2%) and the "asset allocation" (20%) together constitute WHERE, as in where to invest the money. WHERE is less than a quarter of the importance.

According to ASPPA, the most important driver of retirement success is the contribution rate. Three-quarters of the impact is contingent upon how much people invest.

Ironically, the same study found the time spent on the drivers of retirement success were directly disproportionate to their actual impact. In other words, the factors that were least important, like selecting the investments, received the most time and attention, while measures to increase contribution rates that would have made the biggest impact got the least attention.

More recently, the Empower Institute conducted independent research to test these theories with very similar conclusions.[3] They examined four drivers of retirement wealth accumulation to identify "What matters most?": fund selection, asset allocation, account rebalancing, or deferral rates?

The "base-line" performance of their conservative 30-year portfolio was based upon picking bottom quartile funds and staying invested in them over the next three decades (a strategy which actually worked better than picking the top funds 30 years ago and riding them down). The return after 30 years was $205,551.[4]

Asset allocation was much more important than fund selection. The conservative "base-line" portfolio was outperformed by the moderate portfolio allocation ($284,443) and the aggressive portfolio allocation ($333,345).

Account rebalancing had a huge impact on reducing the risk of the portfolio, but actually netted a smaller return than the base-line performance.

Not surprisingly, increasing deferral rates had the biggest impact. The 3% deferral netted a return of $205,551 but even a 1% increase to a 4% deferral showed a significant bump ($274,067) while a 6% deferral rate produced a return better than the most aggressive allocation ($411,101).

Most employers spend too much time on fund selection[5] while too many employees invest far too aggressively and put themselves at far too much risk – the factors of asset quality and asset allocation, respectively, both of which are related to WHERE – when increased contribution rates easily make the biggest difference in retirement success. There is no substitute for simply investing more.

Put simply, the Empower Institute analysis found a 62% increase when doubling the risk of the allocations but a 100% increase when doubling the amount of deferrals without any increase in risk.[6]

One of the line items in the budget is for retirement. It is part of the saucer that catches any overflow from the cup. Managing the budget in such a way that it creates more overflow will have the biggest impact on a successful retirement outcome.

The evilness of averages

The question is *not*, "How much does a person have to invest?" The question is, "How much does the person want to replace in income?" And how soon?

We recommend 70% or more, and we recommend replacing it "as soon as possible" rather than staying in an unfulfilling JOB longer than necessary. Too many models are built on "how much to invest" (defining the contribution) rather than based on "how much is needed." And far too many models are built on the law of averages.[7]

On average, if a person follows this plan, they should be able to retire on time. But rather than the Law of Averages, it should be called the evil of averages. Here is an example of a conversation I do not want to have.

"On average, if you're investing about 10%, you're probably going to be okay. On average.

"And on average, if you started early in your career, you should be okay. On average.

"But last year wasn't an average year ...

"And while putting money in a diversified portfolio like a target date fund is generally a good idea, some target date funds are pretty aggressive and still have you invested in the stock market well beyond your retirement years. On average this provides a nice return, better than a more conservative target date fund. Except, like I said, last year wasn't an average year.

"Your colleagues who retired prior to this year are fine. And younger co-workers who aren't retiring for a while should probably be fine too. They have lots of time to recover and time to prepare.

"But you? Oh, you're screwed. Your money is not exactly gone... it's just in someone else's account. On average the advice we've been

giving plan participants for years has worked well...for most of them ...on average.

"But you lost the genetic lottery because you just happened to be born in a year that placed you at distribution age during a downturn in the market."

I call it the evilness of averages. Contributing too little and investing too aggressively and hoping the averages work out is rather dangerous. I don't like those odds. If a person has a retirement gap to make up it is always better to close the gap by contributing more rather than trying to be too aggressive. And because retirement is a percentage and not an age, there is no reason that age 65 (or any age) should trigger a distribution phase, particularly if the market is below average.

How much should a person invest for retirement?
The recommended amount a person invests (not counting what the company matches) depends on their age and income, since the real question is about income replacement and time horizon (how long they have to build the income replacement). Younger employees can afford to do a bit less while mature employees need to do more – sometimes a lot more.

If the company matches a particular amount, the amount that is matched anchors employee contributions to a rate they should not drop below, but it is hardly the ceiling or goal; the goal is almost always much higher. In simplistic terms it looks like this for an employee who works at a place with a 401(k) match of 5% *if* they are debt free (otherwise, eliminate the debt before moving beyond the 5% match):

1) Contribute 5% to receive the full match,
2) With any overflow, max out the HSA,
3) And with any additional overflow, max out the 401(k).[8]

Assuming the best-case scenario of no debt and excess overflow, the amount of how much to invest ultimately depends on age and income, on how long a person has to build wealth and on how much income they are trying to replace. If they are starting at age 25, they need to invest 7% or 8% or 10%, if trying to replace $30,000 or $60,000 or $90,000 of income, respectively. But if they are starting at age 40, they need to invest 15% of their $30,000 salary (or 17% of their $60,000 salary; or 22% of their $90,000 salary). The investor with less time to build wealth needs to invest more, just as the employee who has more income to replace.[9]

Time is a huge consideration, as time horizon impacts how much a person should save and how aggressively they invest those contributions. The person starting earlier is simply at a huge advantage.

A common illustration from the annals of retirement education is to show the impact of starting early and investing consistently. One such example[10] shows the retirement savings at age 65 for three co-workers (assuming annual contributions of $5,000 and an annual rate of return of 7%).

The first employee invested $5,000 a year for ten years (from age 25 until age 35). After contributing the $50,000 they left the company but left their money in the 401(k) plan as it continued to earn 7% a year. At age 65, their retirement savings are $562,683 without any new contributions in the last three decades.

Another employee started investing at age 35 but continued to invest $5,000 a year until age 65, meaning they invested $150,000 over three decades. Many reasonable people might assume contributing three times as much would produce three times as much at retirement, or at the very least contributing much more might make up for starting ten years later. But few would guess contributing $150,000 would net smaller retirement savings than investing $50,000 just because the first employee had a head start when in fact the second employee has only $505,365 at age 65. Starting early makes a huge difference.

Starting early and sticking with it is particularly impactful. The illustration shares the story of a third employee who started investing $5,000 a year at age 25 (just like the first employee) and continued investing much for four decades until age 65. At the same 7% annual rate of return the $200,000 contribution produces retirement savings of $1,068,048 because of compounding.

Just $5,000 a year but running the marathon consistently without taking any years off.

To Roth or not to Roth? That is the question.

Investing money in pre-tax, tax-deferred contribution or in after-tax, Roth[11] contributions also depends on age and income.[12]

Both pre-tax and after-tax contributions are matched (if the plan has a match) so the only consideration is how a person wants to handle the taxation portion of their retirement income.

To use the figures from the illustration above (a $200,000 investment that grows to $1,068,048) a person who contributes pre-tax contributions would owe taxes on more than a million dollars upon distribution, while a person who contributes after-tax Roth would not owe any taxes upon distribution.

Tax deferred means delaying the tax bill until later, which is generally a good idea. If I owe someone money and they give me the option to pay now or forty years from now (with no additional interest or penalty) I will take the option to pay later. In other words, if the option is to pay taxes on $1 million today or $1 million in four decades, I want to postpone the bill for as long as possible.

But Roth provides a different option. With the Roth feature the option becomes paying taxes on $200,000 today or $1 million later. In other words, with Roth, the earnings are completely tax free (in this case, over $800,000).[13]

Why pay taxes on $1 million when we have the option to pay taxes on only $200,000 ... unless, of course, it makes sense in our situation to take the tax deferred option. It can be a complicated decision, and I always recommend consulting your tax advisor to identify the strategy that best fits your unique situation.

For example, some employees make pre-tax contributions because they need the tax break now. If the budget is tight and there is not a lot of overflow, they might not be able to pay taxes now and still afford to make contributions. (A person deferring 10% only pays taxes on 90% of what they make; a person paying taxes on 100% of what they make might not be able to afford to contribute 10%.)

Other employees make pre-tax contributions if they anticipate smaller earnings. After all, the reason to do Roth is to receive tax-free earnings, so if the earnings were $800 rather than $800,000 the Roth might *not* make sense.

Other employees make pre-tax contributions if they anticipate taxes going down in retirement. If taxes go up in the future, paying taxes now at a lower rate through Roth contributions makes sense. But if taxes remain the same or go down in the future, deferring the payment of those taxes into the future might make sense. (And some people are in a lower tax bracket in retirement than they were during their working years.)

But a person expecting taxes to rise in the future or returns to rise significantly in their account would generally benefit from making Roth contributions. And while there are no guarantees, it is reasonable to assume there might be significant gains the longer the money is invested. When the time horizon is long, and the gap between contributions and distributions is wide, Roth makes sense. This is a fancy way of saying younger investors might benefit more from Roth while those closer to retirement might not.

The Roth 401k has several advantages over the traditional 401k and even several advantages over the Roth IRA.

With the Roth IRA, for instance, a person can earn too much to contribute to Roth[14] while there are no earnings limits in the 401k (traditional or Roth). This could make Roth 401k contributions more attractive for high earners, even if they are older.[15]

In addition, Roth contributions are not subject to the Required Minimum Distribution (RMD) rules so it may make it easier for legacy planning to pass Roth accounts to the next generation.

When I first started in the industry, we used to recommend people invest 10% towards the future … but it is clear that 10% is not nearly enough today. Today, on average, we need to invest 15% to replace our current lifestyle (although it depends on age and income and could be slightly lower or higher depending on circumstances).

Five percent may be enough to get the company match, it may be enough to get started, but it is not enough. In fact, it's not even average. The average savings rate in America today is 6.2%.[16]

It is unlikely to be enough to retire well, and it is unlikely to be enough to replace 70% or more of current income. Most Americans would benefit greatly from simply investing more in their 401k. The good news is there is a relatively painless path to getting on track called "auto-escalation." (If your 401k plan does not auto-enroll and auto-escalate participants at a plan-wide level, ask if you could elect to have your own account auto-escalated for you.)

With the Empower Institute study referenced above, researchers illustrated that increasing contributions had the largest single impact on successful retirement outcomes.

- Raising rates from 3% to 4% increased accounts from $205,551 to $274,067
- Raising rates from 3% to 6% increased accounts from $205,551 to $411,101
- Raising rates from 3% to 8% increased accounts from $205,551 to $503,501

Clearly investing more makes a huge difference ... though some people can't afford to make too big of a jump to get themselves on track. The "auto-escalator" feature allows investors to take small baby steps towards success in a manageable process that, remarkably, is nearly as effective making the huge leap from 3% to 8% (a leap many can't afford to make).

- Raising rates from 3% to 8% increased accounts from $205,551 to $503,501
- But raising rates by just 1% a year, from 3% to 10%, increased it to $489,248
  - Nearly as big an impact as the big jump by taking small steps each year

Here's the deal. It is possible to be a millionaire. It only costs $200,000 and it can be purchased in monthly installments of just $416.67 (less than the cost of the average car payment).[17]

Those who are behind on building their millions may be tempted to make huge bets on risky investments – ironically increasing risk and still not garnering the desired reward – when the path to success is increasing the amount of the installments.

Building wealth is not rocket science but it is behavioral science.

1. I routinely ask this question when meeting with 401k plan participants: How much or where? And the audience almost always chooses the investment selection as the biggest difference maker. Without an exact account, I would estimate it is generally a 3-to-1 split.

2. The ASPPA Journal newsletter: SUMMER 2011 - VOL 41, NO 3. The American Society of Pension Professionals & Actuaries (ASPPA) is an organization of actuaries, consultants, administrators and other benefits professionals.

3. "Defined Contribution Plans: Missing the forest for the trees?" Empower Institute Research, May 2014.

4. Ibid. Please refer to the study for the rates of return and contributions percentages of how they reached this figure.

5. Those making decisions about investments also routinely pick the highest performing funds, which is actually a less effective strategy. Research strongly suggests the better strategy is to pick underperforming funds that increase rather than top performers that decrease, but it goes against human nature for us to invest in what appears to be the loser.

6. The baseline return of a conservative portfolio with 3% contributions was $205,551. Doubling the risk from conservative to aggressive produced a return that increased from $205,551 to $333,345 (an increase of 62.17%) while increasing the savings rate from 3% to 6% increased it to $411,101 (an increase of 100%). The optimum strategy could be increasing the risk AND increasing the savings rate, but the point of the illustration is the savings rate will make the biggest impact.

7. The law of averages is a nod to the false belief that a particular probability is more probable simply because of past circumstances. A common example is the flipping of a coin, that with every 'heads' the likelihood increases that the next flip would be a tails, and yet the odds of flipping heads or tails is a 50-50 proposition, regardless of how many heads or tails were flipped previously.

8. ERISA 402(g) limit.

9. The "Guide to Retirement," 2019 Edition, by J.P. Morgan Asset Management, pages 18-19. The full table is reported in the index.

10. Source of data: J.P. Morgan Asset Management

11. The Roth contribution was introduced with the Tax Relief Act of 1997. Named for Senator William Roth of Delaware, the principal idea was retirement contributions were made on an after-tax basis and grew tax-free. Initially the "Roth provision" could only be found in a Roth IRA, but the Roth contribution was added to the 401(k) and 403(b) with the Economic Growth and Tax Relief Reconciliation Act of 2001 (EGTRRA).

12. I am not a tax advisor and these statements about Roth and after-tax contributions should not be taken to be tax advice. For specific guidance about your unique situation, you should consult your tax advisor and/or CPA.

13. The match on the Roth contributions is still taxable, as well as the earnings on the match from the employer, but the employee contributions and the earnings on the employee contributions are not taxable.

14. For single filers, the phase-out starts at $122,000 in 2019; ineligible at $137,000. For married filers, the phase-out starts at $193,000; ineligible at $203,000.

15. After all, at distribution the Roth money could be left in the market longer while taking pre-tax distributions first, providing more time for higher potential returns.

16. Employee Benefits Research Institute, EBRI 6.2%

17. According to Edmunds, new-car buyers agreed to pay an average of $551 per month for 69 months in January of 2019, nearly a 10% monthly increase from three months earlier, as reported by USA Today, March 1, 2019.

CHAPTER 5
WHERE?

The road to take to building wealth for Repurposement.

The best vehicle to take in the accumulation phase of building wealth is the company sponsored retirement plan (the 401k plan) but there are a number of different considerations to make sure we take the right road: determining the asset allocation, considering the plan defaults, and navigating your own path or letting the professionals drive. Once we have determined the answer to *how much*, the next question is to determine *where* we invest the contribution.

Before we dive into the specifics of where, however, it might be helpful to clarify what we are talking about. There is a huge difference between **Savings** and **Investing**. Savings is for short-term expenses, the cost of maintaining a person's lifestyle in the first half of their life. Investing is for long-term expenses, maintaining a person's lifestyle after Repurposement. Some have confused the two, as evidenced by loans and withdrawals from Investments to pay for short-term expenses. Others have confused Investing with **Speculating**, looking for shortcuts to long-term solutions, often with unrealistic expectations (like doubling the money overnight).

Savings and Investing are part of the saucer; Speculating does not belong in the cup or the saucer.

If 70% of Americans are living paycheck to paycheck[1] we need to build a cushion of several months of income in case the income stream is interrupted. The cushion is what I call Savings. Investing is getting ahead, not a cushion for today but a parachute for tomorrow.

Savings, Investing, and Speculating are three completely different ways to make money work more effectively, using money to make money.

Savings

Savings is putting money aside with a specific goal in mind that is short term. The primary goal in Savings is protection of the principal deposit. The chief concern is security.

To protect the money a person might put it in a high-interest savings account,[2] or money market account, or certificate of deposit (CD). They are okay with slow growth of the money, because growth is not the objective with Savings – it's protection.

Will Rogers, the actor and humorist from the early twentieth century, once said, "I am more concerned with the return of my money than the return on my money."[3] Sometimes 401(k) participants become like Will Rogers towards the end of their journey, because having the market go down just as they are about to step into retirement could be very inconvenient.

Investing

Investing is concerned with the long-term return on money. For this reason, a person will invest in stocks or bonds for the purpose of making money on their money. They might invest in the equity of another company to gain some benefit from the growth of the company, investing directly in the company's stock or in a mutual fund which contains many stocks from many different companies. It is a strategy that works great, if a person has time to let the money grow, because over time, it should grow (that is, in the short-term it might not grow and it might even loss value, but over a longer period of time it often works to the advantage of the patient investor).

The vehicles for investing are stocks, bonds and real estate (or mutual funds of the same). The catch is that each of these come with increased risk, and there is no guarantee of growth, particularly in the short term. Over the long term there should be growth, at least growth that will outpace the rate of return in Savings. This is why cash can be a good place for Savings but not investing, because cash does not outpace the rate of inflation over time.

Speculating

Or a person could throw it all away with something called speculating. Speculating is what a person does at the casino, day trading[4] in the stock market, or playing the lottery. The risks with speculating are enormous because the typical risk-reward equation is not tempered by an efficient market.[5]

Never forget: 'the House always wins!' A casino is a business, not a charitable organization throwing free money away.

A person could fund their Repurposement with 401(k) investments or with Social Security, but the odds are against funding it through the lottery. A person has a better chance of being struck by lightning[6] than winning the lottery. The lottery is a tax on the poor and the less educated. Even a cursory understanding of probabilities and statistics should reveal it is a waste of money. The government keeps holding lotteries because *they* make money ... not because we do.

A person saves with slow growth to protect their money, invests with increased risk to grow their money, or speculates with higher risk to gamble their money.

Everyone likes the safety and protection of Savings, but they want the huge returns (or huge potential for returns) of Speculating. And somewhere in the middle is Investing; it is the proven method of building wealth over time. A person needs to decide if they want to protect their money (Savings), grow their money (Investing), or kiss their money goodbye (Speculating).

This chapter is about Investing, not Savings and certainly not Speculating. Investing is a systematic approach to growing money. It deals with the second and third biggest drivers of retirement success (fund choice and asset allocation). The biggest driver of success is, of course, the investment rate, as in *how much?* But once that question is answered, the next question is *where to invest?* Investing is the art of diversification.

Diversification – Not putting all our eggs in one basket

Even if we know nothing about investments, we probably have heard how important it is to be broadly diversified. At least we have heard the warning about not putting all our eggs in one basket. But what does that mean?

With investments, diversification means spreading the money between and within the three major asset classes. Those three asset classes are stocks/equity, bonds, and cash. Modern Portfolio Theory espouses the concept that to get the best rate of return for the least amount of risk it's important to be broadly diversified. Investors should be properly diversified to garner the return the market yields, to have the sails positioned to catch the wind whichever way it might blow.

To break it down in simplistic terms, CASH is money held in "cash equivalents," financial instruments with high credit quality and highly liquid (easy to access if needed). They are also low risk and low return. Remember in an efficient market there should be a risk-reward trade-off. Taking higher risks should equate to higher returns, at least to a certain point (the efficient frontier) after which added risk does not equate to added return. A good example of "cash" in the 401(k) is Treasury bills (also called T-Bills) which is essentially a loan backed by the U.S. Treasury. It is about as secure as one can be in the investment world. And security is, after all, the objective of cash. High security and low growth is better fitted for Savings than Investing, though most retirement plans have a cash option like a Money Market, Stable Value or Stable Asset. Cash options are built from T-Bills, Certificates of Deposit from the banks, and "commercial paper" issued by corporations (short term loans taken by companies to be repaid quickly with very little risk). The short-term maturities can actually be money repaid as quickly as overnight, but almost always within a year.

And a Stable Asset Fund or Stable Value Fund is like a Money Market, although it often yields a slightly better return and is often backed with some type of insurance for greater security.

Some will mistake security for "safe" as if risk has been removed from the equation, but there is always risk with long-term investing. The risk is cash equivalents is inflation, that the investments will grow so slowly they do not outpace the rate of inflation, meaning they do not keep pace over time with the devalued dollar. A dollar does not buy today what it used to buy, and the difference is the cost of inflation, the rising cost of goods over time. Historically the average rate of inflation is about 3.5% but it has been as high as 13.3% in 1979 and 18.1% in 1946, and as low as -10.3% in 1932 (which was actually contraction and not inflation). Currently, the inflation rate is just below 2%,[7] which is below average. Very few cash instruments will consistently pay more than 2-3%, so if investors are making 1% on cash, and the cash is losing value at a pace or 2-3% a year the investor is losing money.

BONDS are also very conservative but have slightly more risk and slightly higher returns. Bonds are essentially loans, with the investor becoming the "bank" and allowing the borrower (a government entity or corporation) to use their money in exchange for a predetermined rate of return (the yield) when they repay the loan.

The most common types of bonds are municipal bonds or corporate bonds. As with other aspects of the efficient market, bonds increase in returns as they increase in risk, and the risk is determined both by the longevity of the bond and the credit rating of the borrower. A short-term bond borrowed by a highly creditable entity (almost certain to not default) is low risk and low return. The best example, as mentioned above is a Treasury Bill. (Some retirement plans allow employees to invest directly in T-Bills within the bond options or a Money Market which includes T-Bills.) A long-term bond or a bond borrowed by an entity with a lower credit rating produces a higher yield (risk-reward trade-off). The best example is a corporate bond, often called a *High Yield Bond Fund*. And then, somewhere in the middle, is the most often used bond instruments, simply called an intermediate-term bond.

Bonds (money lent to a corporation) are safer than equity (stock held in the same corporation) simply because a company that files for bankruptcy is required by law to pay their creditors first, so while bond holders are often made whole, stock holders are left holding worthless equity shares of a company going out of business.

But bonds, like any long-term investment, has risk. Bonds have credit risk (the risk of not being repaid), interest rate risk (the risk bond prices will fall as interest rates rise), currency exchange risk (if any of the bonds are held in foreign entities), or possibly even the risk of inflation if the bonds grow too slowly. There is also a risk more aptly described as a cost, the "opportunity cost" of how much the money would have made in the stock market rather than the bond market.

The **STOCK MARKET** forms the third leg of the stool, providing investors the opportunity to "own a piece of the business" as a shareholder. The equity shares entitle the shareholder to some of the profits. Stock or equity involves a lot more risk, but it also should involve a commensurate amount of reward in the way of higher returns (at least in an efficient market). Stocks can be divided broadly into two major categories: domestic or international as well as by style. Domestic stock funds are those invested (primarily) in the U.S. stock markets. International stock funds can be invested in developed countries outside of the U.S. or emerging markets in less-developed third world countries. Domestic funds have the least risk, international funds have more risk, and international funds in emerging markets have the greatest risk, and returns should reflect the rewards for taking higher risks.

But stocks can also be understood to be categorized by style: larger capitalization funds investing in larger corporations, smaller capitalization funds investing in smaller corporations, growth funds investing in companies that are still in a growth mode and value funds investing in more established companies deemed to be undervalued.

Market capitalization (also called market cap) is simply the value of a company when taking the number of outstanding shares times the share price at any given time. A company with a market cap of $10 billion or more is considered to be large cap. A company with a market cap of $2 billion or less is small cap. And mid cap funds fall in between these segments. The large cap funds have less risk, and the smaller the capitalization the greater the risk.

Value investing often rewards investors with dividends, sharing the profits each year as the company grows in value. A piece of value investing also involves identifying companies considered to be more valuable than their current price, but the point is value investing is based on the current value (or perceived value) of the company. Growth investing is based on the future value (or perceived future value) of the company. In other words, the investor is investing in a company that is on the rise and may even be an emerging company in the early phase of their assent. The profits the company makes are not paid in dividends each year but re-invested back into the company so it can grow even more the following year. Value investors make money along the way as they hold onto the value stocks, but growth investors make money when selling the growth stocks later at (hopefully) a higher price than purchased. Value stocks are less risk and growth stocks are more risk.

The risk of stocks involve market risk due to market fluctuations, economic risk when the overall economy impacts the value of the companies in the market, currency exchange risk and political risk if the companies involve business impacted by outside nation states, as well as the same inflation risk and solvency risk impacted by other areas of the market. There is always risk involved with long-term investing, even the risk of investing too conservatively (inflation risk).

Diversification is the best way to minimize risk, spreading the investment dollars between multiple funds in the market (large and small, domestic and international, value and growth) because at different times each sector of the market outperforms the others. If an investor had a crystal ball and knew in advance which sector would outperform the others, then they would invest everything in just one segment, but without that prescience the risk of investing everything in the one segment which tanks is too great, so the prudent investor hedges their bet by spreading it around. Not knowing which horse will win the race, it makes sense to put a dollar on every horse in the race. Studies have shown the greater the diversification, even when adding funds that have higher risk, the lower the overall risk of the portfolio. Breaking with conventional thinking, it's also true the broadly diversified approach rewards the prudent investor with higher returns.

The Callan Periodic Table of Investment Returns[8] is often used in the industry to illustrate that each segment of the market has its day in the sun, and every segment of the market can struggle at times. For instance, in 2018 Cash Equivalents (as measured by the 3-month Treasury Bill) had the top performance, so even cash can win the race at times. In 1999, Non-U.S. Equity finished first (as measured by the MSCI world index) but in 2000 and 2001, it finished dead last (and was nearly dead last in 2002 before regaining some footing in 2003). The lesson of the Callen Table is no sector is consistently last or consistently first, they change places constantly, and sometimes take extreme swings from first to worst or worst to first.

Fidelity Investments did an analysis on "Why Diversification Matters"[9] to illustrate how a prudent investor might navigate a changing playing field. First, they listed all of the indexes from best to worst over a 20-year time period[10] and then they asked the question of whether it would have been better to invest each year in the previous year's top performing index or worst performing index. In other words, this year we would invest everything in last year's winner or last year's loser, and then next year we would switch it up and invest everything in this year's winner or loser. The "Best-Performing Index Strategy," based on a $10,000 investment each year in the prior year's best-performing index, produced a portfolio after 20 years of $356,543 (based on $200,000 invested). The "Worst-Performing Index Strategy," based on a $10,000 investment each year in the prior year's worst-performing index, produced a portfolio after 20 years of $411,848 (based on the same $200,000 investment). In other words, it was markedly better to invest in the underperforming funds than the high performing funds, which makes complete sense from a statistical perspective.

The "regression to the means" suggests funds performing below or above average will eventually gravitate towards average (meaning underperformers will rise and top performers will fall). Investing has a lot to do with statistics and probabilities. It makes sense ... statistically.

Unfortunately, it does not make sense behaviorally. Even when confronted with decades of statistics and data, investors find it difficult to pick the worst performing funds. And even when cautioned with "past performance is no guarantee of future returns," the average investor still picks last year's winner, finding it nearly impossible emotionally to pick the loser. And yet, statistically speaking, the odds of last year's winner continuing to be this year's winner is highly unlikely.

In the sports world a phenomenon developed called the "SI jinx" where those athletes or teams appearing on the cover of Sports Illustrated seemed destined for failure. Professional athletes (often noted to be superstitious) even expressed interest in staying off the cover, as if there were actually malicious forces at work. But it isn't voodoo science, it's statistical science. The front cover of Sports Illustrated was reserved for athletes at the pinnacle of their career, and the odds were simply against them continuing to stay on top once they reached the top (or the front cover). It's called the regression to the means!

The valuable takeaway from the Fidelity Investments study was they also illustrated the results of a portfolio after 20 years that was diversified rather than chasing the previous year's winner or loser. The "All Indices Strategy" was based on a $10,000 investment each year, split evenly among nine indexes ($1,111.11 in each). The result of this strategy produced a portfolio valued at $426,230 which beat either of the other two strategies and did so at markedly less risk. It followed what's called a 1/x strategy. In other words, if there are x number of funds (or indexes) an investor simply divides their investments evenly between all possible strategies. This is simple diversification.

Smart diversification or proper diversification (some might say prudent diversification) means each person's unique allocation is customized to their specific needs and risk tolerance. A younger investor can be more aggressively invested to garner greater growth over time, which might mean more money invested towards stocks than cash or bonds, more money towards growth funds than value funds, and so forth. A more mature investor, concerned more about capital preservation and protecting what they have grown, might have the opposite approach. It would not be prudent for both investors to equally divide their investments the same way in a simple diversification approach (1/x).

Remember asset allocation (according to the ASPPA Study cited in chapter 4) is 20% of the factor when determining what drives successful outcomes for long-term retirement planning. The fund selection is only 2% of the equation, but how the investor allocates or diversifies their money between those funds is ten times more important. It is crucial investors get it right. But sometimes the choices can feel overwhelming and some investors will be caught in the paralysis of analysis.

- Should they choose top performing funds or worst performing? (**Correct answer**: lower performing funds, although rarely does the average investor choose this option.)
- Should they choose to be more aggressive if they are younger? (**Correct answer:** generally speaking, yes.)
- If behind should they choose to be a lot more aggressive to make up for lost time? (**Correct answer:** they should choose to invest more.)
- And what happens if they don't make any choice at all?

Defaults – what happens if no choice is made – and auto features

The question of *where* could be the easiest (or hardest) question to answer, depending on the design of the retirement vehicle. It all depends on design and engineering.

A well-designed retirement plan is one which drives itself, instilling confidence in the architect as well as faith in the vehicle's ability to get us to the finish line, a vehicle we could put on autopilot during the long, open straightaway of the accumulation phase by using the auto features.

- Auto-enrollment – investors are automatically enrolled, by default, into the retirement plan unless they specifically elect to opt out of the enrollment process.
- Auto-escalation – investors have their investment rate automatically increased over time to a specific contribution rate target unless they opt out and make an election to stay at a specific investment rate.
- Auto-diversification – investors have their investments automatically diversified for them based upon their age unless they opt out of the diversification process and select their own investments.

Well-designed retirement plans use all three auto features and sets them as the default.

Every plan has a default. A default is simply what happens if a person does nothing. For example, if they do not enroll in the plan will they default into the plan or default out of the plan? If a person works for a company with a properly designed plan, there will be defaults that are beneficial for building wealth.

Defaults can be a way to "dummy-proof" the path to retirement, kind of like putting some bumpers on the lanes in bowling. A person may still need to get the ball rolling, but there are some techniques that can help us avoid the gutters. These techniques are part of the design of the retirement vehicle.

Many retirement plans have a default investment, perhaps called a QDIA, which stands for "Qualified Default Investment Alternative." And the QDIA will probably utilize professionally managed portfolio options to make sure the investments are properly diversified.

To qualify as a QDIA the default investment needs to be a diversified portfolio appropriate for each participant in the plan. The most common QDIA is a Target Date Fund, a comprehensive diversification strategy that maximizes potential for growth when younger while adjusting for the appropriate level of risk as needs change over time (becoming more conservative as we approach the targeted date for distribution). And sometimes the default is a Managed Account (discussed in chapter 6).

The bottom line is the default is (generally) our friend. The employer is required to set up default investments to help us, not hurt us. They are trying to give us some bumpers to keep us out of the gutter.

When in doubt wait it out...don't make any decisions if you are not sure they are the right decisions... and the default will kick in to help if a decision is not made. Assuming, of course, the defaults are designed correctly, it could be the best thing a person can do. And in the majority of circumstances, the default is helpful for employees... although there are always exceptions to the rule.

One exception is if the default investment rate is 0% (in other words, a person is not in the plan unless an election is made). In this case the default is not good because employees are not investing at all.

Another exception is if the default investment rate is too low (although anything is better than 0%). In some instances, the default rate is a low number tied to the employer match. While it may be okay for most people to default at this rate, it may not be good to default if the person is starting late and needs to invest more to catch up. A "non-election" would default them at too low of a rate.

Another exception is if the default investment option is cash.

And another exception is if the default investment option is a Managed Accounts option which costs more (depending on how much more).

But in most cases, the default is helpful. If the default contribution rate is high enough and the default investment option is into a diversified portfolio, the default can be a great option ... no enrollment or election required.

Use the Pros ... or DIY?

A good plan design is to give employees two investment options: the default option into a diversified portfolio and a second option for do-it-yourself-ers to diversify their own portfolio. Option One is to have a professional manager diversify the portfolio for us. Option Two is for us to manage it ourselves in DIY fashion. In my experience about 5% or less of most employees will chose

Option 2 (managing it themselves)[11] which is good, since diversifying investments is probably not what they do for a living. If they were any good at building diversified portfolios, they would probably be on Wall Street, not working on Main Street. In a group of 100 employees maybe five will raise their hands saying they would like to do it themselves (and maybe only 1 of those 5 is actually qualified to do it themselves). Unless a person is working with an advisor who is giving specific instructions on how to diversify the investments, the prudent decision would be to just use the default investment.

A professionally managed portfolio can be a Target Date Fund (TDF), a Target Risk Fund or a Managed Account. Target Risk Funds are decreasing in popularity and use because (a) they are static in risk and the risk tolerance of investors changes over time as they near retirement, and (b) it is not easily automated as the default fund since it requires an election for employees to indicate their risk. (The default is to assume everyone is moderate, which misses the point.) A person's risk tolerance changes over time, especially because "time" is such an important factor in the equation. Our time horizon (how close we are to retirement) changes everything.

In contrast to the Target Risk Funds, the key component of a Target Date Fund is the allocation (the risk profile) changes as a person nears the date of retirement. Most TDFs currently assume age 65, but this will become more fluid as people live longer, as Required Minimum Distributions and eligibility for Social Security is delayed, and as more employees use the funds for Repurposement than retirement (since Repurposement can be done at any age). But the principal still applies that the closer we are to distribution the more concerned we become with protecting the investment than growing the investment.

A Target Date Fund provides a "Glidepath" which slowly de-risks by swapping more aggressive equity funds for fixed income holdings, targeting a particular date to reach the most conservative allocation.

But the target date industry has produced products in many different sizes, and it is often difficult to compare apples to oranges. There are multiple filters through which we might evaluate the appropriateness of each TDF.

First, every Target Date Series starts with a higher equity allocation and ends with a lower equity allocation, called the equity landing, but they all start at different places and some TDFs have an equity landing of only 17% while others have an equity landing as high as 65%. Having only 17% equity at retirement is a big difference from still having 65% of the Portfolio in the stock market at retirement age.

And the industry also does not agree on what "At Retirement" means. Some TDFs have their equity landing at Age 65. In other words, they de-risk to take a Glidepath to age 65, reaching the most conservative allocation at age 65. But there are other TDFs which have their equity landing beyond age 65, some not reaching the most conservative allocation until age 95. The common terminology in the industry is "to" versus "through," meaning the Glidepath takes the investor to age 65 or right through age 65.

Another consideration is how actively it will be managed. Some TDFs have a relatively static allocation. They might start at 100% equity, and then slide down the Glidepath to 90% equity, 10% Fixed Income. And then 80% and 20%, and so forth. The point being, these allocations are predetermined. When a person reaches a particular age, they shift to the next allocation regardless of what is happening with the economy or market conditions. The computer models pre-determine on average this allocation will work for most people over time. (The "evilness of averages" means it often works but does not always work.)

Other TDFs are not static. The allocations are actively managed (sometimes called tactical allocations) and a few are even more actively managed (sometimes called dynamic allocations). A tactical approach allows the managers of the TDF to shift the allocation up or down by 5%-10%, to respond to poor market conditions. In a typical dynamic approach, the managers have even more leeway.

And a fourth consideration is how actively managed the underlying funds are in the allocation. Some TDFs use all passive index funds to control cost, others use all actively managed funds to beat the index (but at a higher cost), and others use a blend of the two.

In February of 2013, the Department of Labor issued guidance on TDFs, on how to select them and on how to evaluate and monitor them.[12] The DOL stopped short of recommending any particular TDF, of course, or even recommending any particular style.[13] But the DOL did stress the importance of regularly reviewing the TDFs and evaluating them for suitability. After all, there is not one size that fits all. An employer should know which TDF style they are offering, and why.

Generally speaking, I recommend a lower equity landing spot rather than too high of an exposure to the market in retirement. I believe a high equity landing puts the employer at greater risk, and a lower equity landing is probably what the employee expects. If a plan chooses the higher equity landing, there needs to be documentation of clear communication employees understand they are still exposed to the market in retirement. For essentially the same reasons, I also recommend a "to" rather than a "through" approach. My experience is most employees think they are in a "to" series if they are in a TDF. Most assume that at age 65 or when shifted to an Income fund in the TDF series they are mostly out of the market.

And again, for the same reasons, I recommend some type of tactical or dynamic approach over a static approach to allow professional management to actually manage the process when needed. Employees in these funds may reasonably assume they are being "managed" rather than left to a static allocation. And lastly, if there are more highly efficient areas of the market that can be covered adequately with indexing why pay more for actively managed funds? A good approach would be a blend of active and passive investments, active when it pays to get better performance and passive to save cost when it makes sense.

One employee told their adviser they weren't nervous about the market dropping because they were in the TDFs. He said, "I'm 66, so my account moved to cash last year."

Unfortunately, his understanding, while not uncommon, was not correct. The TDFs in his company plan did not hit their most conservative allocation until five years after retirement. And even at age 70 they did not take him to an equity landing spot of 0% (all cash.) Few if any TDFs completely move an employee to cash, at any age.

Rebalancing

The professionals also use rebalancing (bringing the amount in each fund back into alignment). They redistribute the money in the allocations to make sure the risk tolerance is still appropriate. It is a hidden secret to lock in gains and build wealth over time. Some will argue it slows down the process of building wealth, and indeed shifting back to a more moderate allocation after a run up in the market can temper some top-side growth, but if the market does not keep running up and falls, the reallocation might shave off a lot of downside loss.

Rebalancing is needed when the appropriately diversified allocation for a person's portfolio is suddenly not appropriate due to market conditions. If they were 60% equity and the stock market does well, they might suddenly be at 80% equity because the stock portion of their portfolio grew. It is nice growth in their balance, but it also might mean they are more aggressive than might be appropriate. If the market continues to grow their balance might continue to grow, but if the market drops it could be a costly drop for them.

The appropriate thing to do is to "rebalance" the account by bringing the allocation back to the appropriate diversification. The way to do this is to sell out of equity, reducing this allocation, and buy into bonds, increasing that allocation. If stocks are up, the investor is selling high; conversely, if bonds have dropped, the investor is buying low. Buying low and selling high is a great way to build wealth.

Each time a person rebalances and adjusts the "floor" of their fixed income it is a little bit like locking in the gains.[14] And if a person is using professional management, like a TDF, the rebalancing is already occurring.

The bottom line is the road to building wealth for Repurposement can be tricky, if we are not careful the vehicle could land in the ditch. In fact, just keeping it on the path requires constant recalibration of the allocation. Ever tried driving a car down the street without moving your hands? Even a perfectly balanced car with new tires will occasionally require a bit of turning or shifting the wheel to keep it on the straight and narrow.

The most valuable asset we will ever have (the 401k plan) deserves lots of attention and recalibration and oversight. The right asset allocation is nearly a quarter of the success factor of whether the vehicle makes it all the way to the finish line. It would be prudent to have a professional driver manage the process if possible (and if it is not cost prohibitive). Most retirement plans give plan participants (the employees) the chance to put the vehicle on autopilot at no additional cost and use Target Date Funds at no additional cost (sometimes for even less cost than the funds in the Core Fund lineup).

And yet, 5-10%, on average, will still try to manage it themselves. My best advice is self-directing should be discouraged at all costs.

Self-directors, on average, underperform the professionals by a tremendous amount. (Fidelity study indicates self-directing could cost 6% or more; Vanguard study indicates 8.42%. No study shows the amateur investor to match the prowess of the full-time professional.) It's absurd that 5-10% of plan participants think they can match wits with the people who manage portfolios every day for a living. While it sounds ludicrous to go toe-to-toe on the court with Michael Jordan, they think they can go toe-to-toe in the markets with Warren Buffett. (Perhaps it's the Dunning-Kruger effect at work, with a little bit of knowledge in the investment area they have overestimated their ability.)

Recent market history provides a warning. December of 2018 was the worst December in the stock market in 87 years (and this in the midst of a very strong economy!) ending 2018 slightly negative or relatively flat (when factoring in dividend growth). Those who were self-directing were often over-correcting, and over-correcting in the market can be just as dangerous as over-correcting on an icy road. With most professional managers cooler heads prevailed and there were not major corrections, but the fears of the average investor were exacerbated by headlines announcing, "the sky is falling."

It's hard when the 401(k) suddenly becomes a 201(k). Those fears are real, and our emotions impact our financial decisions.

January of 2019, however, was the best January in the stock market since 1987. Those who did not make significant changes in December were rewarded with a sharp upswing only one month later. Those who overcorrected in December learned a valuable lesson.

With long-term retirement planning, when it is a marathon and not a sprint, an arduous journey rather than a short-cut to speculative returns – the very best thing the average investor can do is put it on autopilot, using the professionals to drive the vehicle and using all of the auto features available in the plan to navigate the course.

The key is broad diversification, best measured by the correlation of the various underlying investments. The less correlated (the less similar) the better the diversification. In fact, while it might be counterintuitive, adding highly risky stocks to a portfolio does not make the portfolio more risky if the new stocks are uncorrelated to the existing stocks. In other words, if they are independent of each other the risk variance will, on average, cancel each other out.

Correlation (or uncorrelated holdings in the portfolio) are the key, and the professionals managing the portfolio should know how to balance this factor.

It might be necessary to keep an eye on the fuel gauge, to make sure the investment rate is increased over time to produce the desired outcomes; since it is critical to focus on 'HOW MUCH' and since the contribution amount may need to be increased over time, we might not be able to "set it and forget it."

But the best answer to WHERE is definitely to "set it and forget it" – with the pros.

1. According to a CNN Money 2013 survey.
2. This is not the savings accounts at most banks where very little interest is paid, but specifically a bank trying to raise capital that offers a high-interest account for deposits of a certain size. It can be a nice place to "park" some money for a rainy day, and perhaps nice that it requires a transfer back from another institution into your typical banking institution, because it makes it less likely to spend. Just Google "high interest savings account."
3. Quoted in Will Rogers Performer, page 292
4. Day trading is based on speculation in the stock market, specifically buying and selling investment funds within the same trading day. Many times, there are rules designed to discourage this practice because it adds cost while seldom adding value.
5. In an efficient market, according to Modern Portfolio Theory, a person should be rewarded with higher returns when taking increased risk.
6. The odds of becoming a lightning victim in the U.S. in any one year is 1 in 700,000. The odds of being struck in your lifetime is 1 in 3,000 according to the National Weather Service, as quoted in the June 24, 2005 edition of National Geographic. In a lottery in which you pick 6 numbers from a possible pool of 49 numbers, your chances of winning the jackpot (correctly choosing all 6 numbers drawn) are 1 in 13,983,816. That's 1 shot in almost 14 million.
7. As of 2019.
8. https://www.callan.com/periodic-table/
9. https://www.fidelity.com/learning-center/investment-products/mutual.../diversification
10. 1990-2009 was the original timeframe they used, and other 20-year periods have since netted similar results.
11. All things being equal, that is. In other words, when setting up a new plan or forcing an existing plan to re-enroll, I generally see less than 10% choose to "do-it-themselves" but simply introducing the professionally-managed option to an existing plan and not requiring a re-enrollment, inertia keeps many employees in the same investments they have used for years, as DIYers, not because they want to manage it themselves but because people are change resistant.
12. Target Date Retirement Funds - Tips for ERISA Plan Fiduciaries
13. I heard one particular DOL field agent recommend to a group of plan sponsors that perhaps an employer should offer both a "to" series and a "through" series in the same plan, which is awful advice from a behavioral perspective because of how confusing it would be for plan participants. He was not speaking on behalf of the DOL, of course, but offering his own advice. It was just very poor advice.
14. Not to be confused with a guarantee or insured account, because even after rebalancing the account could go down. Rebalancing should decrease risk but does not ensure against further losses in the account.

Chapter 6
Fees!
Which toll roads to avoid on the journey to building wealth.

In the previous chapter we answer the question of 'where,' as in 'Where should we invest?' It is not dissimilar from the question of how to get to Repurposement and which path to take.

The best answer to any similar question is the easy answer: take the direct path. Take the highway or the freeway. Take the easy path, the quickest path from point A to Point B. Apologies to "frosty economists," but avoid the road less traveled.[1]

This is good (Read: "prudent") advice for employers (avoid cute shortcuts, exotic investments, speculative offerings in the 401k). And this is great advice for the employees. Sometimes we assume (wrongly) the answer must be more complicated, but in a relatively efficient market (Efficient Market Hypothesis), given the equalizing impact of averages over time,[2] it seldom pays to be too cute. The best thing the employer (or the employer's Retirement Plan Committee) can do is pick the boring, vanilla funds to offer and the best thing the employee can do is pick a broadly diversified portfolio of these middle-of-the-road options.

But what happens when the direct route, the straightest path, is the most expensive? Prudence requires a most careful cost assessment. Is the direct path worth the added cost?

Locals (which is to say, experienced drivers in a particular city) know which route to take. They probably avoid the longer, scenic route. But they also may avoid the more expensive route, the direct route, when littered with toll booths. If the most direct path comes at a higher cost, is the direct path worth the added tolls?

An inexperienced driver is sometimes left with little choice but to follow their navigational devices and hope the extra cost was worth the investment. Unfortunately, some advisors know this and take full advantage.

On the road to Repurposement there are multiple fees and tolls levied. Some of the costs are fair and reasonable. Others are unnecessary. And some fees are possibly even harmful.

Getting to the destination in one piece, with enough gas left in the tank, could depend on knowing the difference.

When are the fees Fair & Reasonable?

The primary cost of propelling the retirement vehicle is the investment cost, the fees associated with the mutual funds themselves. These are typically referred to as the "expense ratio" because they are illustrated as an asset-based fee (a ratio or percentage of the assets of each particular mutual fund). For example, the expense ratio of a fund might be .20% (sometimes described as 20 basis points). If there were $1,000 invested in a fund charging 20 basis points (bps, pronounced "bips") the actual cost would be $2.

The investment fees cannot be avoided. And many times the fees are considered fair and reasonable.

It is a legal requirement the fees be fully disclosed to every plan participant. (Employees are provided this information, though it is generally more confusing than helpful.) It is also a legal requirement the employer examine the fees at least annually to ascertain whether the fees are fair, reasonable and necessary. (The regulatory requirement is not that they are the cheapest.) Unexamined fees are not fair, reasonable or necessary, no matter how low, because an employer has an obligation to regularly benchmark the cost and the value of services rendered on behalf of their employees.

Investment fees are sometimes fair and reasonable (and since the investment company providing the investments is not a non-profit entity, they are also necessary).

But it depends on the share class. The investments are offered in a variety of different share classes. Generally speaking, those share classes fall within two broad categories: retail share classes and institutional share classes. The difference between the two is like the difference between buying retail or wholesale. Retail share classes are offered to individuals (like individual IRA account holders), they are more expensive, and generally they should not be in a group retirement plan like the 401(k). The best example of retail share classes would be A Shares, B shares, or C shares. Institutional share classes, on the other hand, are offered to large groups of account holders (like those found within an employer-sponsored retirement plan) and they are less expensive. An example of institutional share classes might be an I share or an R share.

Thus any particular investment or mutual fund could be offered in a variety of different share classes (a common example is A, B, C, I, R1, R2, R3, R4, R5, and R6 shares[3]) and the only difference between the ten different shares classes in this example of the exact same mutual fund is the amount of fees charged.

On the one hand, it is important to understand higher investment fees are not always inappropriate. But on the other hand, it is vital to not overpay for the investments.

Higher investment fees from one fund to the next could be negated (or justified) by higher investment returns, though higher investment fees within the same mutual fund (between different share classes of the same fund) could mean a person is overpaying.

For example, if an investor is given two choices (the Orange Fund and the Purple Fund) and told the Orange Fund charges 0.50% while the Purple Fund charges 1.00%, they should look past these charges and inquire about the performance returns. After all, the returns are reported net of the fees so if the Purple Fund is charging twice as much but the returns are significantly higher, it may very well be worth the extra cost for the extra return.

This is different when the Purple Fund has another share class, a lower-cost share class, for the exact same investments. Paying more for the Purple Fund to beat the performance of the Orange Fund is justifiable but paying more for the Purple Fund when there is a cheaper share class of the Purple Fund which still beats the Orange Fund may not be justifiable.

The employer should help monitor these charges and share classes and look out for the best interest of their employees. (This is what it means to be a fiduciary.)

The reason there might be different share classes for the funds with different fee arrangements has to do with how the other costs of the plan are covered. Sometimes the investment fees only pay for the investments and sometimes the investment fees include extra revenue (excess revenue) that pays for all of the cost (in a "revenue sharing arrangement"). Generally speaking, plan costs fall into four different categories:

- **Plan Administration Fees:** expenses associated with recordkeeping, accounting and trustee services.
- **Participant Transaction Fees:** the expenses for optional services provided on an individual participant basis, such as the fees associated with servicing a loan.
- **Investment Fees:** typically the largest expense to the plan and they are broken down as follows: Investment Management Fees (paid to the Investment Managers), Sub-Transfer Agent Fees (paid to the administrator or recordkeeper for providing plan participant account services), and 12b-1 Fees (a marketing fee included in the fund's expense ratio and typically paid to the plan's insurance broker).
- **Advisory Fees:** expenses paid for fiduciary services and investment advice to the plan's fiduciary advisor, sometimes paid in an asset-based fee and sometimes paid as a flat fee. (And occasionally, as referenced above, paid in a 12b-1 commission fee to the plan's broker.)

It sounds like a lot of fees, and much has been made about the fees in retirement plans, but in total the fees are often quite reasonable. In other words, when adding together the investment fee and all of the different service fees, the cost is still generally less expensive than investing in an IRA (*Individual* Retirement Account) because the large trust account of a 401(k) has the extra benefit of "cost-sharing" within a larger investment vehicle. The aggregated larger pool of assets allows lower overall costs than the smaller assets in an individual account, hence wholesale costs rather than higher priced retail expenses.

The question is how these shared expenses are paid. In today's environment of full disclosure, the best business practice is increasingly to itemize each expense so the cost is fully transparent rather than "hiding" the fee within a higher-priced investment share class. When an investment company collects more revenue than it needs in a higher priced share class, extra revenue is shared with the other service providers to pay their cost (revenue sharing).

Option A, for example, charges X amount for the investments, Y amount for the administration, and Z amount for advisory services, while Option B might charge XX for the investments without charging a separate amount for admin or advisory services, enough extra to cover all of the costs after the investment company shares the extra revenue.

PHD. Consulting was recently hired by a company paying a higher expense ratio for recordkeeping services. By moving to a lower cost share class, the plan participants saved a tremendous amount of money even though they were now charged a per head fee to pay for recordkeeping. It required some explanation, because plan participants initially objected to seeing a hard-dollar cost assessed to their account. They never saw a separate charge previously but obviously the service provider was not working for free previously. Once they understood the overall cost had been reduced, they were accepting of the per head fee.

Another trend to control investment fees within retirement plans is the movement towards Collective Investment Trusts (CITs). The mutual funds described above (with A shares and R share classes) are registered investment funds, registered with the Securities and Exchange Commission (SEC) under the Investment Company Act of 1940 (hence the nickname "40 Act Funds"). While moving from retail share classes to institutional share classes and from actively managed funds to passively managed index funds can reduce the cost of the 40-Act version of these investments, moving to a CIT of those same investments can be a way of controlling costs even further.[4]

CITs are tax-exempt, pooled investment vehicles sponsored and maintained by a bank or trust company. CITs are exempt from the registration and filing requirements of the Securities Exchange Commission (SEC) and independent boards are not required, they generally have lower administrative costs. Office of the Comptroller of the Currency (OCC). CITs have been around since 1927 but have grown significantly in popularity within defined contribution or 401(k) industry.[5] In fact, their popularity has grown so quickly that more than one-quarter of the $5.5 trillion 401(k) market was invested in (CITs) in 2017.[6]

CITs are not possible in individual contracts and are often only possible in larger retirement plans. It provides an additional way for large plans to control cost, offering a lower-cost option from the traditional mutual fund.

CITs are regulated by the OCC, IRS and DOL; mutual funds are regulated by the SEC.

CITs are available to retirement plans but not the public; mutual funds are available to the general public.

CITs have no 12b-1 fees and greater flexibility on fees; mutual fund fees are determined by share classes and may include 12b-1 fees.

CITs are generally less cost; mutual funds are generally more cost.

But CITs still have some cost. Plan fees are a necessary evil. The investment companies and service providers are operating a for-profit business. And while much has been reported (and misreported) about plan fees, many times the fees are not excessive, unfair or unreasonable. It is important to keep an eye on the share class and not overpay for investment returns, but because the returns are net of the fees, the fund fees are seldom the issue.

Are any of the fees unnecessary?

I will never forget the day in my MBA Finance class when our professor was painted into a corner. He had just completed a lecture on the benefits of actively managed mutual funds over passively managed mutual funds. He admitted both have their place, but in explaining how the markets work he was clearly trumpeting the value of active management. The class asked the professor where he invested his own retirement money. He tried to avoid the question but eventually acquiesced to admit he put his own money in...index funds.

Index funds are mutual funds that track with a particular index rather than trying to beat the index. One example is a large cap index like the S&P 500 Index or a small cap index like the Russell 2000 Index or a bond index like the Bloomberg Barclays US Aggregate Bond Index. Managing an S&P 500 index is easy, something any 5th grader could pull off. The recipe looks like this: obtain a list of the 500 companies in the S&P 500 (a simple Google search) and invest money in each, weighted appropriately for what percentage they are of the total S&P. It is called "passive management" because there are no management decisions to make. Passive management does not overweight towards one of the 500 companies they have more faith in or ignore any of those 500 companies based upon market research. In fact, there is no research involved.

Consequently, it is extremely cheap to manage.

An actively managed fund, by comparison, is not trying to mirror the index but beat the index, and for the market research and analytics required to beat the index, they charge a premium in fees.

The raging debate is whether it is worth the extra cost for active management or if these fees are unnecessary.

One of the hallmarks of Modern Portfolio Theory (MPT)[7] is the market is efficient and it is not possible to beat the market. If the market is efficient (if, over time it yields a predictable rate of return based upon the actual profits of the underlying companies, not an unpredictable return based upon speculation) then passive investing makes sense. In other words, why pay a manager a high fee to beat the market. An efficient market will seldom be beaten in the long run.

For purposes of retirement planning, the 'long run' is the key. In the short term, markets can be very inefficient and open to speculation, but in the long term they should even out and yield the return consistent with the actual value of the companies within the market.

It is a raging debate because there are really smart economists and finance people on both sides of the debate. Some argue passive management beats active management the majority of the time. Others admit the index might outperform active management most of the time but the outperformance of active management in those few years is so great it warrants the case for active management.

My educational background is in Behavioral Psychology and Behavioral Finance. When I think about long-term investing, I think it has more to do with statistics and probabilities.

I also think the finance industry is built upon an 'illusion of skill.'[8] Billions of stocks are exchanged every day, and generally speaking, the buyers and sellers have the exact same information. The transactions do not (largely) take place because the buyers and sellers have different information, but because they have different opinions about that information. The opinions are impacted by "judgment biases" such as the *Dunning-Kruger Effect* whereby individuals of poor understanding overestimate their abilities. That is to say, the more ignorant people are about a given topic, the more certain they are right, the worse their judgment and the more inaccurate their overestimations.

Think of it like this: in a closed market there is always someone on the other side of each transaction; there must be a buyer for every seller (and vice versa). One person is convinced it is the time to sell, but another person is convinced it is the time to buy. How can they both be right? The price of a given mutual fund (or the price of the stocks within the mutual fund) are supposed to take into consideration the actual value of the company based upon all of the information available. If the price is accurate, no one should gain or lose by trading it, because it is a "fair price."[9] In other words, those who think the price is high and want to sell it and those who think it is low now but likely to rise and therefore want to buy it, would not gain from the exchange. If the price is fair, all of this buying and selling is nonsense.[10]

 After all, the more efficient a market is, the more accurately priced the holdings within the market, and the less likely anyone is to beat the market. A judgment bias which leads some to try to beat the market could have the opposite effect of garnering significant losses.

As previously stated, a person's 'Retirement Readiness' has very little to do with their allocations and even less to do with the actual fund choices within the allocations[11] I focus on the largest single factor in 'Retirement Readiness' which is how much a person invests. Chasing the myth that a fictitious blend of the right investments is going to make the difference seems futile. Stick to working on what we know makes a difference: investing more.

Admittedly there are some portions of the market that are more efficient than others and, in those areas, passive investing probably makes sense (because it is unlikely, statistically speaking, to always beat the market over time). But in other areas of the market an investor may be rewarded for selecting active management and paying higher expense fees because there can be additional gains to be found in an inefficient market.

The key to long-term retirement planning is less about knowing the difference (which efficient sectors call for passive investing and which inefficient sectors reward the added cost of active management) and more about broad diversification in an allocation that touches all sector (using active and passive management).

The key to long-term investing takes us back to my original advice to just use the appropriate professionally managed option, like the Target Date Funds, one that rewards a more aggressive equity allocation when young and de-risks as we age. Even if passive management wins the day most of the time, active management wins enough and wins by enough of a margin that going 100% index is probably not wise or prudent.

Just make sure the professionally managed option in the 401(k) plan is not overcharging.

Some fees are even harmful

Some fees diminish retirement savings and delay the date for retirement, particularly fees that come 'off the top' of the account, after the performance returns. Those top-line fees cannot be justified with higher performance because they directly reduce the investment returns.

A fund that reports a return of 10% and a fee of .50% actually had a return of 10.5%, because the 10% return is reported net of the fees. But a fund with a 10% return, a .50% expense ratio, and a 1% management fee only nets 9% to the employee because the management fee comes off the top, directly decreasing the money for plan participants.

The best example of this is Managed Accounts, a professionally managed portfolio that sometimes assesses a fee.[12]

Some employers, in seeking a professionally managed option within the retirement plan, chose a specific type of professionally managed product called Managed Accounts (note the capitalized description of "Managed Accounts" to designate a specific type of managed account, different from other managed options like Target Date Funds).

Not all Managed Accounts (MA) are bad ... but many are suspect.

Some MA are professional allocations of the investments also available in the Core Funds within the plan and offered as the default or QDIA at little or no additional cost.

But sometimes the list of Core Funds does not include the same investment options as those within the MA portfolios, and may even include investments with lower performance, making it impossible for an employee to match the performance available within the MA.[13]

And sometimes the MA come at an additional cost. This is particularly concerning if MA is set as the default. Defaulting employees into an option that costs more raises a serious fiduciary concern.

There are a few recordkeepers that provide MA at no cost, using the underlying Core Funds to build the portfolios. But there are some RIA firms charging excessive top-line fees that are harmful to plan participants. These are the toll booths to avoid.

The U.S. Government Accountability Office (GAO) issued the findings of a study (GAO-14-310)[14] that questioned whether there are any benefits of MA within an employer-sponsored retirement plan. The primary concern was the exorbitant fees for this type of professionally managed portfolio (particularly given there are many MA programs that do not charge and given there are other professionally managed portfolios like Target Date Funds that can be very low-cost options for diversification). The study reviewed approximately 95% of the MA providers and found the benefits did not outweigh the cost (and the cost varied dramatically from vendor to vendor). Regulators have warned employers not to use MA. If an employer persists in offering them employees should avoid this expensive alternative.

In some cases, employees are defaulted into the MA program (or sold the program)[15] and charged an outrageous amount, like 1%, to manage the portfolios. The GAO and DOL have concluded even a 1% difference in fees can mean as much as a 28% difference in returns over the lifetime of the plan.[16]

The MA program should be free of extra cost to the employee. And if the MA charges more than 50 basis points (0.50%) it is likely causing serious, irreparable damage, deteriorating the amount of wealth needed for Repurposement.

What about hidden fees?

The retirement plan industry has moved towards greater disclosure and fee compression. The initial movement towards disclosure was beneficial to all parties (except service providers overcharging). But the movement towards fee compression has netted some unsavory side effects.

All service providers in the industry are in the business to make a profit. Full disclosure of fees and services encourages healthy competition that should benefit the consumer in an open (and fair) market. But some service providers have created new revenue sources to supplement lost revenue, while other service providers have simply passed the cost on to other partners or to the end consumer, sometimes in ways designed to skirt the disclosure regulations.

Employees engaged with building wealth should seek to understand the Total Plan Cost and how this compares to measurements of fair, reasonable and necessary.[17] Knowledge is power. Understanding nothing is free and cheap is not always better, employees simply need to understand the value of what they receive (value as determined by cost and services).

The traditional way to price retirement plans was to charge one all-encompassing fee, wrapped up inside the expense ratio, and removed prior to returns on investments. Few if any employees or employers understood the actual cost. Technically it was one fee because it was an expense ratio with a higher share class fund which included enough excess revenue to pay everyone else.

The movement towards disclosure broke up this arrangement in a way that itemized the different service providers. In pulling back the veil everyone could see (theoretically) what everyone else was making.

The employer has two responsibilities related to fees in the retirement plan (neither of which are "provide the cheapest option"). First, the employer should make sure the fees are fair, reasonable and necessary, appropriately priced for the services rendered. And secondly, the employer should make sure the employees understand the cost and value. Nothing should be hidden.

In one example, employers may have the opportunity to reduce fees if the cost is broken out as separate line items but have an increased burden to communicate with employees who now see a charge on their statements that was not there before. The employees were previously paying more but did not know it. Now they pay less but they see the cost.

Was ignorance bliss? Should the employer have remained in the more expensive option rather than moving to a cheaper option that caused controversy with a charge on the statement? Does not the employer have the burden for disclosure, for clear and concise communication, either way, whether remaining in the "one-hidden-fee" approach or breaking out each fee on the statement?

Complicating this a bit is the idea of ancillary services or additional revenue sources that some providers create. For instance, if the employees are told the expense ratio, the admin/recordkeeping/custodial fees, and the advisory fees, should they not also be told the additional management fee (if the MA has a fee) in the context of Total Plan Cost? Should not the employees understand how additional fees compare in an analysis to overall plan costs? And if one of the service providers (the recordkeeper or the financial advisor) receives additional revenue from using their own investments, should this not also be reported? At the very least it creates a huge conflict of interest because the recordkeeper or financial advisor is unlikely to fire themselves and remove their own funds for underperformance. It is also deceptive if the employees or employer is led to believe the service provider is only receiving the fee they have disclosed and not reporting additional revenue received from using their own funds or their own MA program.

Everything should be brought into the light.

Every employee who is a participant within a 401(k) plan should receive full disclosure about all fees within the plan.[18] And the employers who sponsor the retirement plan must receive full disclosure of all fees from every "Covered Service Provider"[19] so they might determine (at least annually) whether the plan fees are "fair, reasonable, and necessary."[20] This means the employer has a legal responsibility to evaluate the fees to benchmark the cost to make sure employees are not overpaying.

After all, a person generally gets what they pay for, and cheap is not always better, but employees should understand the fees and avoid the excessive fees. Too many toll booths along the road to Repurposement can sabotage the journey.

1. Robert Frost poem published in 1916: "The Road Not Taken."
2. That is to say, short-term investing is markedly different in trying to turn a quick profit, but in long-term investing like retirement plans the averages work out to reward basic diversification in a moderate portfolio.
3. Many investment companies use A shares or I Shares or R Share class, although some companies create their own nomenclature such as N or K.
4. A common myth is CITs are always cheaper than their 40-Act mutual funds. While most CITs are less expensive, there are exceptions.
5. Specifically using 401(k) since 403(b) plans narrowly define qualified investments to be 403(b) annuity contracts or 403(b)(7) custodial accounts (more commonly known as mutual funds). In other words, CITs are not generally allowed within the 403(b) retirement plan unless it is a non-ERISA 403(b) with an exemption under Title I of ERISA (such as a "church plan").
6. This is according to Cerulli Associates, Plan Sponsor Magazine, September 10, 2018.
7. I've made several references to MPT. There are (2) components to MPT: the assumption of correct pricing and the assumption we can't beat the market. As a normative benchmark for understanding free markets, MPT adds some value and perspective. But as a descriptive model of how the world really works, we must understand that sometimes the price is not always right and sometimes it is possible to beat the market. The question is at what cost? Investors who accept MPT and invest in low-cost index funds should not be faulted. The markets are often efficient, but not always efficient. I agree with some but not all of MPT.
8. This is not my original idea. I believe I heard Dr. Daniel Khaneman say this.
9. Chapter 24 of Dr. Richard Thaler's book *Misbehaving* (2015) is titled *"The Price is not Right,"* a reference to the two major components of the Efficient Market Hypothesis, being (1) you can't beat the market because there are "no free lunches" and (2) you can't profit from mispriced securities in the market because "the price is always right."
10. Brad Barber and Terrance Odean published a paper titled "*Trading is Hazardous to your Wealth*" in which their decade-long study of more than 60,000 investors revealed that, on average, the most active traders had the poorest results while those who traded the least had the highest returns.
11. The ASPPA Journal newsletter: SUMMER 2011 - VOL 41, NO 3. The American Society of Pension Professionals & Actuaries (ASPPA) is an organization of actuaries, consultants, administrators and other benefits professionals.
12. Not all MA assess a fee. Several major recordkeepers and service providers offer MA at no cost, building diversified portfolios from the underlying Core Funds. But some RIA firms charge a management fee for MA.
13. I believe there could be a bit of a conflict of interest if the employees are "forced" to use MA because their only other option are sub-par investments in the Core Funds. Or, at the very least, it seems manipulative or coercive to force the use of MA.)
14. Read the full report of the government's warning about MA programs at https://www.gao.gov/products/GAO-14-310
15. Sometimes the employee enrollment meeting can become a "sales meeting" for the employees as they are "sold" on the idea of selecting the MA option rather than self-directing. The advisor or enroller should not stand to profit during the employee education meeting.
16. "*A Look at 401k Plan Fees*," updated August 2013, p. 2. Available at www.dol.gov
17. There are a number of independent sources to benchmark fees, relying upon *The 401k Averages Book* or the *Fee Benchmarker® Advisor/Consultant Fee Comparison Report* is more objective, and prudent, than relying upon the service provider's self-reported benchmark of their own fees. If you have questions about the fees in your retirement plan contact me or another third-party professional for a second opinion.
18. This is required under ERISA 404(a)5
19. A Covered Service Provider is anyone to whom they are paying $1,000 or more.
20. This is required under ERISA 408(b)2

CHAPTER 7
RISK
Navigating the road hazards along the journey.

There are healthy fears and unhealthy fears; warranted fears and irrational fears. Fear can be an important part of our defense mechanism, but it can also be a crippling and debilitating response to the world.

Personally, I have no interest in jumping out of a perfectly functioning airplane. Nor will I jump off a bridge with a rubber band. I do not have a fear of heights...just a fear of falling to my death. I think these are reasonable fears. However, others have a fear of even getting on a plane in the first place (aviophobia) or a fear of heights (acrophobia).

I am trying to encourage everyone to get in the retirement vehicle known as the 401(k) ... but some Americans have a fear of even getting in the car. (Vehophobia, perhaps?) It is true the path to Repurposement can have a few road hazards, but we cannot let this keep us from completing the journey.

Long-term retirement planning already involves risk, whether it is the risk of market fluctuation with risky investments or the risk of inflation with conservative investments. All investing involves a degree of risk. But there is no reason to assume more risk than necessary, and the common mistakes discussed in this chapter exacerbate the risk to create road hazards that make an already difficult journey even more challenging.

Missing the ride

Forty-five percent of Americans do not have access to an employer sponsored retirement plan,[1] what we call 'savings-made-simple.' This is where the money comes right out of the paycheck before they even have a chance to spend it (or miss it), and gets deposited for them in a 401k (or a similar vehicle) on their behalf. We have a major coverage gap in America with half the country unable to participate in a traditional 401(k) plan, which is why decision makers in Washington DC are considering a number of solutions to offering more access.[2]

But of the other half of Americans who have access to an employer sponsored retirement plan, only 66% of eligible workers participate in one.[3] About one-third never get in the car! Perhaps their retirement plan was not set up with the proper defaults to simply put them in the car if they did not actively elect to get in the vehicle. Or perhaps it is something deeper.

Some employees have a fear of losing money. Most of us are loss-averse to some degree. This is not an irrational fear. Someone who is hyper loss-averse may be super conservative with their investments. That's okay. What is not okay, though, is doing nothing with your money.

Some employees have a fear of the stock market. Like my father, playing the stock market was perceived as gambling. But again, investing is not speculating. There is a huge difference.

I understand loss aversion, the fear of the market, and the fear of failure. But the alternative is sticking our heads in the sand and hoping for the best … or hoping Social Security can bail us out.

If a person has a retirement vehicle at work it is an opportunity and it is a test, an opportunity to provide for their family and their future, but a test of their discipline and determination. Will they have the strength to stay on budget and direct the overflow towards their future. It's a test.

The first question on the test is, 'Will you participate?' and there is only one right answer to this question. (The answer is yes. Yes, you should participate.)

The second question on the test is, 'How much will you participate?' and getting the contribution rate right is paramount to whether it works. I recommend doing no less than the employer matches and using the overflow budget to invest even more after covering basic needs and paying off debt.

There is a fear of not doing enough, but the biggest road hazard is doing nothing. A person who does not invest will not be able to repurpose and apart from Social Security may not be able to retire.

A person who never gets in the vehicle will fail without a major adjustment in lifestyle (i.e., a major reduction in lifestyle).

Letting emotions take control of the wheel

Others get in the vehicle, but their driving is so bad it constantly puts them and their portfolio at risk.

My mom's mom (we called her "Big Mama") lived in L.A. (that's Lower Alabama, not Los Angeles). Big Mama produced most of her own food, mostly out of necessity. She was ahead of the farm-to-table trend some restaurants have adopted. Almost everything she consumed was grown in Big Mama's backyard.[4]

When she wanted to serve chicken for supper, she literally grabbed one from the back yard. There were two options, both of which Big Mama exercised without hesitation or remorse. She could grab one of the chickens and "ring her neck" or she could separate the head from the body and watch her run around the yard "like a chicken with its head cut off."

Both experiences left me traumatized as a young boy.

But today I am sometimes reminded of those headless chickens running around the yard when I see employees bumping back and forth through market fluctuations. The idea of the head being separated is a great analogy because it seems like far too many investors "lose their minds" when their emotions become involved.

Investment risk is real...but it is also real easy to resolve in an appropriately diversified portfolio. The key is to spread the risk, diversify the investments, and then step back and not micromanage the process. Putting all the eggs in one basket is dangerous, of course, but quick movements in the portfolio can break the eggs just as easily. Like overcorrecting on an icy road, overreactions are not prudent. When it comes to investment changes the mantra is *slow to hire, slow to fire.*

The key is to be *appropriately* diversified. If the fluctuations in a person's account are such that they are tempted to make changes or make corrections, they are probably not in the appropriately diversified portfolio. They might need to be in a more conservative portfolio so they are not tempted to make adjustments.

Imagine yourself in the passenger seat of the retirement vehicle with a professional driving the car. If the driver is driving too fast or too aggressively for our comfort level, it is perfectly reasonable to request a more conservative driver. But it is not reasonable or safe, in most instances, to reach over and grab the wheel. An aggressive overcorrection is more likely to send us into the ditch. Being in the right portfolio means it is the right fit for our risk tolerance so we are not tempted to take control of the wheel.

The market (and our portfolio) will, of course, fluctuate. This is normal. If a person has a fear of roller coasters (coasterphobia) or fluctuations in their 401k (investorphobia)[5] they just need to ride the coaster that is more conservative, so they are less queasy.

After all, a down market is not necessarily bad news. When the market is down, it means the price of the investments in the market are down. If we hear the price of goods is down at the store we consider this great news. It's a sale, a buying opportunity. But when we hear the price of investments is down in the market we panic. The media misreports this as awful news. The lead story on the evening news is never, *"Great News today! There was a big sale on Wall Street!"* Instead, it is always *"The market crashed today … the sky is falling … millions of Americans lost their retirement savings."*

The fearmongering is only due to the fact that fear sells more papers.

A down market is a buying opportunity. I want to buy in a down market. Unfortunately, most people do not approach investing with this rational framework and our emotions put us at risk of making irrational choices. When people hear the market is up, for example, they want to get into the market. Conversely, when they hear the market is dropping like a lead balloon they move out of the market and into cash. It does not make sense to buy high and sell low. Our hearts are telling us that, not our heads. But we sometimes act as if our heads are separated from our bodies, like the chickens.

When the account balance is down, we still have the same number of shares, but the price per share has dropped. We may have an "unrealized loss" or a loss on paper, but it is not a "realized loss" unless we make a trade and sell those shares at the lower price. If we do this the loss becomes real, we lock in the loss, a mistake we may never recover from.

In 2008, we experienced a Recession during the Financial Crisis. The market dropped precipitously. Many Americans had their 401(k) reduced in half to a '201(k)' because the media hammered home the 'Chicken Little' message about the sky falling, and many Americans lost half their retirement savings when they moved to cash. They did not lose their retirement savings because the market dropped, because those who did nothing had their accounts return and surpass the previous market high. They lost their retirement savings because they grabbed the wheel and overcorrected, therefore landing in the ditch.

I was among the fortunate. I did not cash out or run for the hills. I held on and I did nothing. If I had been sitting in cash prior to the drop I might have even pushed more money into the market because it posed a buying opportunity. But I was in a broadly diversified portfolio, so I did absolutely nothing.

I did nothing because I knew I was young and had plenty of time. I did nothing because I knew it would be disastrous to sell low. I did nothing because I ignored my emotions of fear and I kept a long-term perspective. I did nothing and my account came roaring back over time and far surpassed pre-Recession highs. The only people who did better than me were those like Warren Buffett who could afford the extra cash to push into the market and buy low. After all, when everyone else was selling, someone had to be buying. Buffett likes to say when everyone else is buying, he likes to be selling, and when everyone else is selling, he likes to be buying.

Behavioral Finance teaches that our emotions often get the best of us. Greed causes us to buy high and fear causes us to sell low, and our emotions drive us into poverty.

The worst advice is *'Buy high, sell low. Buy high, sell low. Repeat 'til broke.'* It is the advice our hearts and our emotions are giving.

Down markets can be great news...if we have plenty of time.

Speeding tickets & moving violations create a road hazard

Unfortunately, many of us misjudge the time, causing us to drive the wrong speed limit.

A lot of investors underestimate the amount of time it will take to prepare themselves for Repurposement. When they are young, they do not take it seriously, and with each passing year of delay the journey becomes much more difficult.

Consequently, a lot of Americans fail to drive the proper speed limit. Young employees drive too slowly (failing to invest enough, early enough) while older employees drive too fast, trying to make up for lost time and missed contributions with overly aggressive allocations.

Both driving too slow and driving too fast can cause an accident. Both are dangerous. There is no magical way to circumvent the slow and steady approach of starting early and running the marathon with purpose.

Building wealth is not complicated... but it is also not easy. It requires some discipline and at times some hard choices. It is hard. Not quite like trying to nail Jell-O to a tree... but it's close.

If a person started contributing late for retirement the solution is to invest more, a lot more, to get more fuel in the vehicle: To do whatever they can, make whatever sacrifices they can, and get the fuel to jumpstart the journey.

They might even have to sell stuff. Anything to increase investments.

But a person needs to avoid the risk of taking on more risk than they should. Anything but increase the risk of the portfolio beyond reason.

As an example,[6] if a person is using the Target Date Portfolios, rather than choosing the year their age would have defaulted them into (like the Target Date 2025 fund) they could choose a more aggressive profile and opt for the 2035 fund or the 2045 fund (investing as someone younger than themselves might). This keeps them in a diversified portfolio and it skews them towards a more aggressive profile. (After all, if they did not start investing early enough, their actual retirement date might be closer to 2035 than 2025 anyway. Retirement is not an age.)

But no year (2045 or 2055 or even 2065) is going to close the gap like increasing the contribution rate.

The solution is to invest more (a lot more), only adjust the investment risk slightly (avoid the risk of taking on too much risk), and plan on working longer. Retirement is not a number or an age; retirement is a percentage. A person is ready for Repurposement when they can replace 70% or more of their income and live on 70% or less of their income.

And if they are starting late, this is unlikely to be something a person can do at 65. If they got in the vehicle late, they are going to arrive late. And they may possibly need to adjust expectations of what Repurposement looks like.

And they must avoid the potholes in the next chapter. The margin for error is now much smaller and they cannot afford any setbacks at this point. Even a small pothole could knock them completely out of alignment.

1. According to the US Bureau of Labor Statistics, 2017
2. The most recent solutions involve expanded guidance around the Multiple Employer Plans (MEPs), particularly Open MEPs, and Association Retirement Plans.
3. According to the Department of Labor, from *"Adding Automatic Enrollment to your 401(k) Plan"*
4. I should say Big Mama was not particularly large, and I am not aware she ever found the title particularly offensive. In the south Big Mama is a term of endearment. I am told in the other LA, it is considerably more offensive and much less endearing.
5. I made up this phobia. To the best of my knowledge, the other phobias and fears described in this chapter are real, but investorphobia has no empirical basis or known cure. Investorphobia is not a real phobia … but perhaps it should be.
6. This is just an example of how a person might dial the risk tolerance within their portfolio up or down and should not be construed as investment advice. As each person's unique situation and time horizon and risk tolerance is different, they should seek personalized investment advice from a qualified financial professional.

CHAPTER 8
POTHOLES
Pre-retirement distributions that knock out the alignment.

Seems like each area of the country has their own unique season. It's part of the local flavor.

In Minnesota they have four seasons: Almost Winter, Winter, Still Winter, and Road Construction.

In many places throughout the south (Alabama or Louisiana, for example) they have one season: it is always college football season.

I grew up in Florida where we had one season: some variation of hot and/or humid. And when I moved to Kansas City I learned about a new season we had never had in the Sunshine State: Pothole Season. Harsh winters take a toll on the roads which in turn take a toll on our vehicles. In the spirit of tolls to avoid or road hazards on the way to Repurposement, potholes could potentially cause the most damage.

Each winter the roads in Kansas City are treated with salt, which eats through the snow and ice and pavement. And then the pavement is mercilessly scraped to remove the snow and ice and salt. The roads are destroyed, and our vehicles are knocked out of alignment. It's almost like winter is in cahoots with the auto repair shops.

Potholes and pitfalls in a person's retirement account could also knock out the alignment or might completely wreck the car. Successfully reaching Repurposement involves avoiding the potholes of these pre-retirement distributions at all costs.

Potholes related to job changes

When my dad stopped working, he retired from the only real job he ever had. He spent four decades delivering mail. He was briefly in the Air Force and then he briefly worked as a mechanic on airplanes, but mostly he worked for the U.S. Postal Service. He only had one job... but then he is part of the 'Builder Generation.'[1]

I am part of Generation X.[2] I have changed jobs multiple times and I completely changed careers once (from vocational ministry to the retirement industry). And one change is probably on the low-side for most people in Gen X.

Those in Generation Y (or the Millennial Generation) switch jobs nearly as often as they change outfits with dozens of different jobs as the norm.[3]

The sense of loyalty to any particular employer (or even within a particular industry) is an archaic idea. The workforce is constantly in flux. And each time a person leaves their job they have a decision to make about their retirement plan.

The good news is 401(k) plans are completely portable. (Just a few decades ago an employee would be leaving their non-portable pension plan and having to start over if they changed jobs.)

The bad news is 401(k) plans are completely portable.

We get to take them with us and do whatever we want to do with them. There is nothing to keep us from cashing them out every time we change jobs. Essentially, we have the ability to do to ourselves what the old pension system used to do, hitting a disastrous re-set button each time we terminate employment.

And unfortunately, there is nothing to protect us from ourselves; nothing standing between our own short-sightedness and the impulsive purchase. And since the government benefits in taxes and penalties when we cash out early, we cannot expect Washington to be tightening this loophole anytime soon.

This pothole could knock a person completely out of alignment or could even land them in the ditch. The goal with this vehicle is simply to keep it between the ditches and to keep the dirty side down. But emptying the tank every time we change jobs is disastrous. Even if the amount accumulated is small, it really does add up over time if we leave it in there. The upside reward of leaving the money invested when we leave the job outweighs any short-term gains.

There are four options when a plan participant terminates employment, one option will send them careening into a ditch, but two other options could knock them out of alignment. Only the fourth option is ideal.

The wrong decision, the harmful decision, the one which sends them into the ditch, is cashing out. First, they will pay taxes and (if they are under 59 1/2 years of age) they will pay penalties. Secondly, they will have to start over and rebuild the retirement account at the next job. Remember the illustration of the person who started investing early and how beneficial it was to have the early deposits working for them? Imagine if they kept cashing out and removing those early deposits each time they changed jobs? They would sabotage their own Repurposement!

So, what are the other options?

They could take a rollover and roll the money into an IRA or they could leave the money in the 401(k). But both options could knock them out of alignment if they are not careful.

Remember the previous discussion about fees and different share classes (the difference between retail and institutional shares)? Rolling a 401(k) to an IRA is so prevalent it seems acceptable, but it could be harmful if the IRA charges higher fees.[4] The fees could diminish the growth of the account. Generally, the best place to accumulate wealth for retirement is inside a 401(k) plan. Do not roll the account into an IRA prior to retirement.

But keeping the money in the 401(k) after a person leaves could also knock them out of alignment if they move on and forget they have the account, forgetting to keep an eye on it or misplacing the account altogether and failing to update their address when they move.

Believe it or not, millions of Americans have misplaced millions of dollars intended for retirement over the years.[5] In fact, the DOL is ramping up its audits of retirement plans with missing participants, putting pressure on plan administrators to locate former employees or beneficiaries to receive the benefits they are owed.[6] Almost like the missing children initiatives, perhaps we need to put missing participants on milk cartons.

If keeping the money in a 401(k) (not an IRA) is the best option, the question is, 'In which 401(k) plan should the money reside?' And the simple answer is a person should keep the money in the plan they are currently contributing to, not the one they left. If their new job has a retirement plan, they should start contributing as soon as they are eligible and rollover the 401(k) from their prior job. Having accounts in multiple places makes it harder to keep all the investment objectives aligned, while having the accounts together makes it easier to keep track of them (and keeps them off the side of the milk carton as a missing participant, which is certain to knock them out of alignment).

Roll it forward to the next company 401(k) if this is an option, or, if it is not an option, leave it in the previous company 401(k) plan, if this is an option. (Though leaving it in the old plan is not always an option.)[7]   Try to avoid rolling it into an IRA, and under no circumstance cash it out.

1. The best thing is to roll the old 401(k) to the new 401(k).
2. The next best thing is to leave it in the old 401(k).
3. The next best thing is to roll it to an IRA.
4. The worst thing is to cash it out, to pay taxes and penalties.

Ironically, another casualty of frequent job changes is a provision that was supposed to be helpful for producing healthy participant outcomes. Auto-enrollment is great for getting new employees into the plan, particularly when coupled with auto-increases that raise their contribution rate over time. But if they keep changing jobs and keep being auto-enrolled, they are probably being kept at a lower contribution rate than what is appropriate. If this happens several times, an employee might never get to the percentage they should be investing. (Obviously, the new employee could enroll themselves at a higher percentage, but few do, so the auto feature designed to make it easy and help employees might actually harm those who change jobs frequently.)

Some newer auto-enrollment features are beginning to take age into consideration. For example, employees in their 20's might be auto-enrolled at a smaller percentage (and auto-increased) but those in their 30's, 40's and 50's might be auto-enrolled at a higher percentage, giving them a higher starting point even prior to any auto-increases. JPMorgan conducted an analysis that determined appropriate starting points for different age groups.[8] They recommend those who are just starting to save today and in their 30's invest between 8%-13% (if earning between $30,000-$90,000 a year, respectively); that those in their 40's invest between 15%-22% (given the same income range); and that those in their 50's invest between 31%-47% (given those same ranges). Of course, the point of the illustration is the longer someone delays starting the more they need to invest, because the percentages they suggest are unrealistic and unattainable. The person making $90,000 and investing 22% exceeds the IRS contribution limit[9] while the person making $90,000 and contributing 47% exceeds even the allowable catch-up limit.[10]

The pothole is not changing jobs but what people do with the plan at their last job, and what they do with the plan at their new job.

Are 401(k) loans really harmful?

Pre-retirement distributions are preventing many American workers from building the wealth necessary to ever get ahead, and this includes borrowing money from the account, even if it is done with the good intentions of repaying it. Nearly a quarter of plan participants (26% according to a 2018 Aon Hewitt study) have outstanding loans against their account.

Loans from the 401(k) plan generally mean the employee is selling part of their investments, converting the money to cash which they remove from the account, and then repaying the loan over time at an interest rate that is supposed to allow them to regain some of what they might have lost from being out of the market during this time. While repaying the money is better than not repaying it (a loan as opposed to a distribution) it is still not an ideal solution for money management. Taking the money out of the market and out of the plan retards growth and puts the employee back several steps in planning for Repurposement.

The unfortunate thing is some employees have the impression loans are a reasonable option, or at the very least not harmful to long-term savings, because the money is put back. And admittedly, given the other option of withdrawals that are not paid back, it does seem like the lesser of two evils. But considering why people take loans in the first place[11] the logic behind 401(k) loans seems a bit specious at best. Taking a loan from the 401(k) is very costly.

Removing money from the market where it could be earning money creates an Opportunity Cost (what it would have earned if it had been left alone).

Processing the loan generally incurs an expense from the service provider, which is the Administration Cost. And in addition to the cost of processing the loan, it is repaid at an interest rate of generally 1%-2% over the prime rate. Ironically, the repaid interest is the reason provided by some for why the loan is not particularly destructive to long-term goals for retirement. After all, some say, 'I am making 2% on my loan, so I am making something' as if taking the money out of one pocket and putting it in their other pocket is "making money." The loan borrower pays themselves the interest, so they are not "making money" on their money … they are paying themselves.

There is also a Tax Cost (i.e., lost tax efficiency). Loans are repaid with after-tax dollars, creating the situation of double taxation for borrowers.

If a person defers $100 (deferring the taxes on $100 until they retire) and then take a loan, the loan is repaid with after-tax dollars. So, $100 contributed in pre-tax dollars is now repaid with after-tax dollars, meaning the employee paid taxes on the money they put back into the plan. And then taxes are assessed again on the same $100 at retirement, on distributions going back to the deferred basis of $100. The impact is double taxation.

To put it another way, someone in the 25% tax bracket would need to earn $125 to repay $100 of the loan.

And this is assuming they repay the loan at all. Many times employees leaving a company have outstanding loans in the

401(k), which, upon termination, become distributions. The unpaid loan balance is immediately subject to taxes when it becomes a distribution, as well as a 10% penalty if the borrower is under 59 ½ years of age. And the overall efforts to retire on time are set back if the loan is not repaid.

How destructive are loans to the Repurposement process? One financial institution (Bankrate.com) provides an online tool to help employees calculate the cost of borrowing by illustrating how much they will lose. If everyone understood the cost better most would avoid the damage cause by this pothole.

Are 401(k) loans really harmful? Yes! There is an opportunity cost, an administration cost, a tax cost, and a distribution cost on unpaid loan balances, all of which could cost us our chance at retiring on time.

Potholes related to sales and annuities

Obviously, the advice above about what to do with the retirement plan may be different from the advice other advisers provide. In fact, it is quite possible an insurance broker advises an employee to rollover the 401(k) into an IRA because it will benefit the salesperson. It may or may not be in the best interest of the employee (due to the higher retail expenses) but it is always clearly in the best interest of the salesman. And therein lies the conflict of interest.

A huge pothole on the road to retirement is having salespeople in the break room meeting with employees. The employee meetings should not be conducted by salespeople, insurance brokers or commission-based financial advisers who could impact their income if employees buy their services. Sales meetings disguised as Retirement Education and/or Financial Education is a huge conflict of interest and places the employer and the plan at risk of significant fiduciary liability.

After all, if an employee is required to attend a retirement plan meeting at which some product or service is pitched, they may feel coerced into buying the product.

When advice is offered by someone who stands to profit from the acceptance of the advice, get a second opinion. Find someone who does not have a dog in the fight and ask them for guidance.

If an adviser is charging a retirement plan a fee and the adviser convinces an employee to roll their money out of the plan and into an IRA that charges the employee more and pays the adviser more, it poses a clear conflict of interest.

At issue is not whether the IRA is beneficial for the employee (it may be in some rare instances). And at issue is not whether the fee is a fair price for managing an IRA. At issue is whether it is reasonable for the plan adviser to give advice to do the rollover, conflicted advice which clearly profits the adviser.

Under ERISA 406(b) it seems clearly to be a conflict of interest and possibly even a prohibited transaction.

The excuse sometimes given for why the IRA rollover makes sense despite the extra cost is the desire to hold an investment with retirement assets that is not available within the 401(k). And the example provided is generally some type of annuity.

Annuities are guarantees, like buying insurance for our money. And like most insurance products, annuities are sold, not bought. They involve high commission structures and fees which handsomely reward insurance salespeople and are sold to unsophisticated investors who are scared into a transaction based on the fear of running out of money in retirement.

Annuities are insurance for the money that require "locking up" the money for a specified period of time and receiving very small returns on the investment because most of the returns are paid in commission back to the insurance salesperson. The advantage of the annuity is they pay something (and something is better than nothing). They are guaranteed to protect principal and guaranteed to not lose money. Employees who are fearful of negative returns or running out of money before they die are willing to accept very low returns for this guarantee. It provides peace of mind for not losing any principal.

Peace of mind is important, and in some cases, it may make sense for employees to "buy" this expensive peace of mind for *some* of their money … but investors need to understand the cost.

It is unfortunate an entire industry was created around fearmongering and few employees really understand the cost of these purchases.

Many retirement plans allow "in-service" distributions once an employee is 59 ½ years of age. Distributions are always allowed (albeit not always advisable) when there is a separation from service, but in some cases, employees can take distribution when still "in service" with the company if they are 59 ½. Brokers and advisers regularly exploit this loophole and try to convince employees to roll out of the plan at 59 ½. But this is rarely advisable.

Don't take my word for it. Ask an accountant. Ask an attorney. Ask anyone who does not stand to profit from the purchase of an annuity, what they think about leaving the plan to buy an annuity.

I could fill this chapter and many volumes with horror stories about annuities. For example, the person who was duped into exchanging their life insurance policy to buy an annuity, and then their spouse died and they were left with nothing,[12] or the retirement plan that was charged extra fees because a few large account holders were tricked into cashing out their 401(k) to buy what they thought was a safety net.[13] Or the scores of individuals I know who were scared into buying an annuity at the bottom of the recession only to exchange the growth on the other side for a small guaranteed return that was largely diminished because of the excessive fees.

Some advisers hold employee education meetings with a list in hand of those plan participants over age 59 ½. The primary objective is to educate them about how to separate them from their money, to roll them out of the plan and into an annuity, playing on the fears of the employees.

Several regulatory efforts from Washington DC attempted to resolve these issues. The Department of Labor's Fiduciary Rule would have made these rollovers more difficult, but this provision was stalled and later struck down. As the Securities and Exchange Commission works on their own version of a new Fiduciary Rule, there are now legislative efforts to include provisions for in-plan annuities to help employees intent on finding a safety net from seeking more expensive options outside the retirement plan.

At issue is whether an adviser working with an ERISA retirement plan like a 401(k) has to assume a fiduciary role and do what is in the best interest of plan participants. (It is amazing we needed regulations to require this!) Also at issue is whether plan advisers are able to "cannibalize" the retirement plans they serve by capturing IRA rollovers that pay them higher fees than if money had stayed within the plan.

The bottom line is ERISA already requires retirement plans operate for the *sole benefit* of plan participants and that decisions made by employers and service providers be in the best interest of plan participants. A new fiduciary rule or regulation should not have been required to emphasize a plan advisor is a plan fiduciary and that they are always required to operate *solely* in the best interest of plan participants. The only debatable point is whether moving employee accounts into annuities is in the best interest of plan participants, but pre-retirement distributions are rarely advisable.

Potholes related to mistimed distributions

Timing is everything. And unfortunately, it is something we have little control over.

We can control how much we invest and where we invest it, but we have minimal control over timing. We have no control over how much time we have left until retirement any more than we have control over how much time we have left to spend the money.

Nor do we have control over what the market is doing when we decide to exit the plan. Although we do have control over when and how we exit.

One of the biggest potholes is exiting the plan at the wrong time. If it happens to be a down market in the year we were planning to take distribution, we may never recover. If we begin withdrawals in a down market, we may very well run out of money before we die, which would be incredibly inconvenient.

J.P. Morgan Asset Management did a study illustrating the importance of the sequence of returns, showing that the risk of negative markets was considerably greater at or just before retirement. In fact, according to J.P. Morgan, "when saving for retirement, the return experienced in the early years has little affect compared to growth achieved through regular savings.[14] However, the rates of return just before and after retirement when the wealth is greatest can have significant impact on retirement outcomes."[15]

Money is contributed to the retirement plan in a process called "dollar cost averaging," which means it goes in intermittently at various values in the market, as the market rises and falls, and the average of a fluctuating stock market actually helps the accumulation process. Unfortunately, few investors remove their money in the same systematic approach, dollar-cost-averaging their withdrawals as they did their contributions. And if employees take all of their money out at the same time, they had better hope it was the best day (the high point in the market) for doing so. In fact, if they take a withdrawal in a down market, particularly early in the distribution phase, the result is not dollar cost averaging but *dollar cost ravaging.*

Dollar cost ravaging illustrates the timing risk of withdrawals.

Investors would be wise to be broadly diversified in non-corelated asset classes and to be flexible on when they take distribution. A good advisor[16] can guide a person through this process. One example might be taking Social Security payments first and not removing money from the market if the timing is wrong, or only taking a small portion of what is needed if the market is down when Repurposement had originally been planned.

Spending the same amount in retirement regardless of the market performance or taking the same distribution amounts as it is indexed for inflation (increased slightly over time) could result in an unsuccessful outcome. Investors should consider adjusting the distribution rate or spending strategy, based on market conditions, to help make the money last longer. Of course, if employees are debt free and have worked the entire program as described in this book they will have the opportunity to be much more successful in the distribution years.

My advice is plan participants need to transition (mentally and otherwise) to a "Repurposement" state of mind, taking back control of the situation. A person has options if they are repurposed into a job they enjoy doing, a job they would not mind doing and could keep doing if it is not the right time to stop collecting a paycheck and take distribution. Invest as much as possible; invest in as broadly diversified portfolio as possible; transition over time into something you enjoy doing in case you do not want to take distribution during a particular market cycle; and keep the options open.

And debt free living gives us options.

A person has a certain window, based upon age, when they should file for Social Security,[17] but a person does not have a window when they must repurpose; particularly if their work is fulfilling and they are living on purpose. A person could repurpose anytime, as soon as they want. Or they could wait to not do so if the market is down and market conditions are not favorable. After all, retirement is not an age; it's a percentage.

Mistimed distributions are an easy pothole to avoid if a person leaves themselves options.

The road to Repurposement – building the wealth necessary to be repurposed at any age, whenever a person can replace 70% or more of their income and live on 70% or less of their income – is a road is marked with many potential potholes, so many it may feel more like driving through a minefield.

Successfully completing the journey may depend on our ability to avoid distribution mistakes when changing jobs, early withdrawals and loans along the way, expensive annuities in our path, and mistimed distributions in bad market cycles. Most of these potholes can be navigated with the help of the plan advisor but sometimes, particularly as the date of Repurposement approaches, it will require the help of a skilled pilot.

1. The Builder Generation, also called the Silent Generation, is traditionally those born in the 18-year period from 1927-1945, although some argue it starts in 1924 and runs through 1945.
2. This is the generation of those who came after the Baby Boomers. The Boomers were created in the post-war boom, the 18-year period from 1946-1964. Gen X is the 18-year period from 1965-1983.
3. A Bureau of Labor Statistics news release published in March 2015, indicates younger baby boomers started the trend, holding an average of 11.7 jobs, though 27% held 15 jobs or more, and this number is projected to grow. Forrester Research predicts that today's youngest workers will hold twelve to fifteen jobs in their lifetime. The full report is available at https://www.bls.gov/nls/nlsfaqs.htm#anch41
4. The retail share class funds in an individual account are almost always higher than the wholesale institutional share class funds in the larger retirement plan account.
5. There's no exact measure of how many unclaimed benefits are out there. But a report released last year by the Government Accountability Office states that between 2004 and 2013 more than 25 million people left at least one retirement plan behind when they left a job.
6. Assistant Secretary of the Department of Labor, Preston Rutledge, who oversees the Employee Benefits Security Administration (EBSA) said at the 33rd Annual Conference of the Employee Benefits Institute that missing participants were one of the major areas of focus for this current administration.
7. If the account balance is above $5,000, their former employer cannot force them to take it. But the employer can force them to take distribution of a smaller account. And if their new employer does not have a plan they can roll it to, they may have to accept an IRA rollover.
8. JPMorgan, Guide to Retirement 2019, page 18.
9. The 402(g) limit for 2019 is $19,000 and 22% of $90,000 is $19,800 so this would exceed contribution limits.
10. The catch-up limit for 2019 is an additional $6,000 raising the total limit to $25,000 but 47% of $90,000 is $42,300.
11. According to a 2018 survey from TIAA, the primary reason employees provided last year for taking loans was to pay off debt.
12. This is a true story based on a personal account retold to me by a CPA firm. The "victim" was unfortunately one of their clients.
13. This is also a true story based on a retirement plan I served at one point in my career. An unrelated insurance agent was able to obtain a list of every plan participant over 59 ½ years of age and held meetings to convince employees they needed to move their accounts or risk losing everything. Enough account holders made the move, resulting in a drop in the plan assets and a subsequent increase in plan fees for those who remained in the plan, since the plan fees were based upon asset size.
14. To further illustrate the point that it really is not about *where* but *how much*, at least in the early years and particularly during the accumulation phase, though one could argue the *where* becomes much more important at the end of the journey and during the distribution phase.
15. J.P. Morgan Asset Management, Guide to Retirement 2019 Edition, pages 39-40.
16. That is, a good personal advisor, someone who is a Fee-only advisor and registered as a Certified Financial Planner™ (CFP®), is someone who understands how to advise clients regarding taxation and social security and distribution strategies. This is a very different skillset and expertise from the Certified Plan Fiduciary Advisor (CPFA®) who only specializes in consulting on employer-sponsored retirement plans, like 401(k) plans.
17. Choosing the backside of this window when it is Full Retirement Age, not the front side of the window when a person is settling for less money.

CHAPTER 9
HOW TO SAFELY EXIT
Using a Pilot to land the vehicle in Repurposement.

Arriving at our destination means we built the wealth necessary for retirement, Repurposement, and recommissioning. We got in the vehicle and put in enough fuel to keep it moving down the road. We grew the investments through a broadly diversified portfolio, avoided unnecessary toll roads, steered clear of road hazards, and avoided the potholes. We kept the vehicle on the road, between the ditches, dirty side down, just like we talked about. Thanks to a lot of blood, sweat, tears, and some hard choices, we accumulated some wealth.

But that was the easy part.

The accumulation phase is much easier than the distribution phase. At least it is easier to get the accumulation phase right; and it is much easier to mess the distribution phase up. The distribution phase requires more expertise and guidance than the accumulation phase. Accumulating the money is like learning to drive; while it's challenging for new drivers it becomes routine and easy over time. But distribution is more akin to parking the vehicle, and even seasoned drivers can struggle with parallel parking.

This chapter discusses how to exit the highway without crashing, how to find a pilot to land without wrecking. It would be a shame to come this far only to crash and burn. This book is not about the distribution phase of life, about whether the "drawdown rate" should be 4% or 5% to not run out of money. This book is about the recalibration, repurposing, reorienting and accumulation segments of the journey. But I would be remiss if we failed to at least address the difficulties of the deboarding process in this final chapter, just as investors might be remiss if they try to navigate this one on their own.

My advice is to practice deboarding a few times, a "distribution drill" of sorts to see if the vehicle is ready to complete the journey. And then, if ready to exit, find a pilot to exit safely. Without a few practice drills it is hard to know if the timing is right, and without a pilot at the controls it is hard to do it right.

Distribution drills to test the timing for Repurposement

It is possible to buy a lot of things sight-unseen, and online shopping has completely changed the retail experience. Thanks to Amazon, nearly anything can be delivered. But while it is true we can now buy cars and homes online (thanks to car vending machines like Carvana and virtual tours of houses) the trend is still towards buying smaller ticket items sight-unseen while preferring to "test drive" the big-ticket items.[1]

Retirement is the biggest big-ticket item we will ever buy. It does not make sense to purchase without trying it on for size, without at least taking it for a test-drive. It's hard to 'test drive retirement' for most employees, although a skilled pilot can assist in modeling how much can be distributed, when to take the distribution, and how long the payouts might need to last based on life expectancy. The modeling is complicated, and most Americans take the leap into retirement 'flying blind.'

In fact, more than 10,000 Americans a day[2] make the transition: they make the biggest purchase of their lives with little preparation or warning or practice, without trying it on or taking it for a test drive or even seeing it.

When they started with the company decades ago, they were given a chance to "buy it," not just to make a significant down payment, but to start in motion a payment plan which would eventually buy their retirement. The payment plan, paid in installments over forty years, allowed them to purchase something of incredible value. And rather than paying interest by stretching the payments out, they actually received interest, compounded returns on their investments.

The million-dollar question is whether we are on track. If retirement were an age, the answer would be easy. (i.e., we are "on track" to reach age 65 in x number of years.) But retirement is not an age; it's a percentage. Are we on track to replace 70% or more of our income? And how is 70% income replacement going to work? Can we live on 70% income replacement? (The answer is no, if we have outstanding debt.)

A number of studies have attempted to answer the first question of whether or not we are on track, although only we can answer the second question of how 70% income replacement is going to work for our family within our current lifestyle.

When I started working in the retirement plan industry the "experts" used to say a person needed a million dollars to retire. Later the number was inflated to two million dollars. Missing in either figure was substantive guidelines based upon age and income. J.P. Morgan Asset Management published a guideline for "Retirement Savings Checkpoints" that is much more helpful.[3] According to their research, the amount needed grows as we age, but it also grows (as a multiple of household income) as we earn more. The simple reason for this is lower-income households will qualify for higher income replacement through Social Security, so they don't need as much to replace their current lifestyle.

For example, a person who earns $50,000 a year needs to have invested 2.4 times their current household income by the time they are 45 years of age, 4.1 times their current income by the time they are 55, and 6.7 times their current income by the time they are 65.[4]

In comparison, a person who earns $100,000 a year needs to have invested 3 times their current household income by the time they are 45 years old, 5.6 times their income by the time they are 55, and 9.6 times their income by the time they are 65.[5]

And 9.6 times $100,000 is only $960,000 which falls short of the recommendation by some to have a million dollars saved. One million dollars would be 10 times $100,000; 6.67 times $150,000; 5 times $200,000; and 4 times $250,000. By way of illustration, according to J.P. Morgan, this is more than a person needs if earning $100,000 and approximately how much a person needs who is earning $150k, $200k, and $250k at ages 55, 47, and 42, respectively.[6]

For our purposes the question is whether or not this is going to work. If this is how much is needed to be on track to replace 70% or more of our income in retirement, the question is whether we can live on 70% or more. How is it going to "fit" in our lifestyle? A distribution drill provides a FREE 90-day trial before we purchase it.

According to the Employee Benefits Research Institute, the national savings rate (the percentage of money invested by Americans every year) suggests Americans have spent between 98.4% and 93.8% of their incomes over the last 20 years. (Although more recently the contribution rate in America has hovered between 5.8% and 6.2%, there was a period over the last two decades when it was as low as 1.6%.)[7]

How in the world is someone supposed to retire when they have not shown any propensity for fiscal restraint, spending nearly every penny they made? How can a person living on 98.4% adjust to living on 70% of their income in retirement?

And some Americans have lived on even more than 98.4% of what they make. Some have lived on more than 100% of what they make thanks to the ability to use fake money and charge it to a credit card.

Retirement is not a math problem. Some pundits suggest if we invest X amount of dollars for Y amount of years and earn Z amount of interest, then we will be able to retire. This is retirement, not Algebra.

And X, Y, and Z does not change our behavior.

Nor does X, Y, and Z account for the last forty years (when we were supposed to be preparing for retirement) when we became addicted to spending. Stepping off the precipice into retirement without adequate preparation is a good way to break a leg.

Five years in advance of making the transition, start running parallel budgets (a detailed budget of how to manage money this year, and a rough outline of how to manage it in five years). Kind of like a current Operating Budget and a future Retirement

Budget. And each year the Retirement Budget will become more defined, more detailed, and more similar to the Operating Budget.

When a person is about 9-12 months in advance of the Target Launch Date for Repurposement, shift the current income to a figure that will more closely resemble income in retirement. For example, if the goal is 70% income replacement (as I suggest) then set the retirement plan contribution at 30% to force yourself to live on only 70% of income.[8]

Run this trial for about 90 days to get the feel for what it might look like to live on slightly less in retirement.

Six months prior to the launch date a person should have had at least one of these 90-day trials. The results of this experiment will either confirm they are on the right path or encourage them to change their flight path. It may reveal they need to adjust their expenses (addressing outstanding debt) or that they simply need more practice to adjust to it.

I don't know an easy way to say this so I will simply be direct: the result of the 90-day trial might be that they need to move the launch date back.

If a person concludes they need more income than their savings can provide the answer can be a bitter pill to swallow. There are only four possible answers to the question:

1) They can't retire;
2) They can't retire now;
3) They need to re-evaluate what they really need in their overflow budget; or
4) They need to find a second job for income in retirement.

Blindly removing too much income from the retirement nest egg (more than the 5% most recommend) is not the same as driving an extra 50 miles with the fuel light on and hoping for the best. Ignorant perseverance could lead to irreversible consequences.

My recommendation for a distribution drill is a 90-day trial to shift as closely as possible to the projected income replacement levels. The goal is to help adjust the flight path for a successful outcome: to encourage more investing and/or less spending and/or postponement of the launch date.

Stepping into retirement need not feel like a free fall. The final year before Repurposement might look like this:

1) 9-12 months in advance, run the trial.
2) Evaluate. Adjust the budget or adjust the launch date.
3) If major adjustments were made, re-run the trial.
4) 3 months out, shift to the Repurposement budget.
5) And on the launch date ... repurpose, recommission, and relaunch the next chapter of life.

Ironically, a 2010 study conducted by Allianz found 61% of individuals fear running out of money in retirement more than death itself and yet nearly two-thirds of retirees do not have someone they consider to be their financial advisor based on a 2011 LIMRA report.

This is too big of a step to take without some practice just as it is dangerously foolish to take without the help of a trusted advisor. Experience tells us in order to learn something we need frequent practice and immediate feedback. Unfortunately, most of us won't have multiple opportunities to get this right.

The importance of having a Pilot on board

One of the most fascinating jobs (in my opinion) is that of a Harbor Pilot (also called a Port Pilot or Maritime Pilot). They do not have to be at sea for weeks at a time. Ships cross the ocean for weeks without a pilot, but once they arrive at the destination, the pilot's job is to park them.

In fact, the captain's job, on approaching the port, is to hoist the G Signal Flag which literally means "I require a pilot."

Each port has local pilots familiar with the unique currents and depths and uniquely trained in navigating vessels through dangerous congestion to bring them into the docks. A pilot boat (or in some cases, a helicopter) brings the pilot aboard before the ship enters the harbor. The captain steps aside and lets the pilot drive. Even if the ship's captain is a regular visitor in that port, they can never match the expertise of the local port's pilot. The pilots do the parking, taking the boats in and out of port. And, on average, these pilots make between $250,000 and $500,000 in salary.[9]

The ship's captain, in most ports, does not have a choice. It is called "compulsory pilotage." The captain can stand by, but the pilot has the wheel.

What interests me about this is the seasoned captain, the person who has been at the helm for nearly the entire journey, is required to step aside and allow the local pilot to take charge. The captain is much more familiar with the boat, but the pilot is the expert in bringing it in.

If only 401(k) plans had compulsory pilotage.

I have never piloted a ship, but I have piloted a plane. I have flown enough to be dangerous, or that is, enough to know where the real dangers lie.

The dangerous part about flying is not flying...it is landing. It might feel scarier at 5,000 feet or 10,000 feet (or 35,000 feet on a commercial airliner) but it is much more dangerous bringing it down. The plane I flew was navigated by foot pedals. Toggling the pedals up and down controlled the wheels when it was on the ground. Coming in fast on the runway and steering the plane with extremely sensitive foot pedals was very uncomfortable for me.

Almost anyone reading this is likely capable of piloting a boat in open seas or a plane at 5,000 feet or even a 401(k) plan when they are thirty years away from retirement. In fact, it is so easy that those vessels are often put on autopilot in open space. Getting it off the ground or out of port requires some skill but getting it back on the ground or back in port is challenging.

Bringing a plane down is hard.

Not hard to bring down (gravity helps) but hard to bring down safely.

Bringing the vehicle in without crashing is no easy task either, and a mistake could be very costly. (A piloting error with the Exxon Valdez cost $5 billion when it ran aground at Prince William Sound in Alaska.)

This chapter is about the importance of finding a pilot to bring the retirement vehicle safely into port. It is about finding a pilot we trust to not run it aground. Everyone needs a pilot.

The Merchant Shipping Act of 1894 still defines a pilot to this day: "any person not belonging to a ship who has the conduct thereof."

A person may be the captain of their own ship, but may not be qualified to be the pilot, particularly at this point in the journey.

I enjoy the opportunity to help employees find the right pilot. I am not a pilot, nor am I a financial advisor. I am a plan advisor, a plan fiduciary advisor.[10]

I know enough about the financial advisory business to help people find the expertise, but it is not my business, it is not my core competency, and it is not where my expertise lies. In fact, I have a personal financial advisor I meet with to manage my own financial affairs. Doctors do not treat themselves; they maintain their own health by submitting to the care of another. Similarly, to maintain the financial health of my household, I submit to the coaching, guidance, expertise and care of another.

I think it is odd so many plan participants, lacking even a hint of expertise, try to pilot their own vessel without the skill and advice of another. Their primary experience with financial investments is participating in the 401(k) for a few decades. But that experience hardly qualifies them as an expert. A prudent person would not try to wing it at this point. There is simply too much at stake.

And it is an error in judgment to think only the wealthy need an adviser. Everyone needs a pilot.

Remember also the Dunning-Kruger effect says over-confidence causes those with the least ability to mistakenly think they can manage it themselves while those with the highest capabilities are most often prone to find a pilot.

I am often asked, by plan participants, if I can help them with this transition. I always seek to refer them to someone, helping them find a trusted advisor. I do not manage individual accounts, and I am not qualified to pilot the vessel into port.

I enjoy offering impartial advice on which pilot to work with because I am not in this business of personal advising. I like to help employees get started, hunting with a shotgun when the primary goal is to propel as much money in as broadly diversified a fashion as possible. But at the end of the journey a person would be wise to find someone who knows how to hunt with a rifle, who has more pinpoint accuracy on shaping the portfolio.

I want to make sure the wealth I have helped the employees build is properly stewarded and piloted now that we have completed a successful journey. As Richard Thaler writes in *Misbehaving*, "When the stakes are high and the choices are difficult, people will go out and hire experts to help them. The problem… is that it can be hard to find a true expert who does not have a conflict of interest. It is illogical to think that someone who is not sophisticated enough to choose a good portfolio for her retirement savings will somehow be sophisticated about searching for a financial advisor…. Many people have made money selling magic potions and Ponzi schemes, but few have gotten rich selling the advice, 'Don't buy that stuff.'"[11]

Identifying the right pilot

If a person is not in the financial industry, they may not realize there are many different types of advisors and many different ways in which those advisors offer financial guidance. The different models determine who the advisor is working for and what kind of advice to expect.

In short, the pilot is really working for whomever signs their check.

Many people have operated under the allusion their adviser was working for them, that their adviser was always doing what was in their best interest. In fact, they might have even believed the law required them to do what was in their interest.

ERISA does not just require an adviser to act in the best interest of plan participants and their beneficiaries; ERISA requires advisers to act SOLELY in the best interest of plan participants and their beneficiaries.

But the financial industry and insurance industry has worked diligently to avoid doing this for many years, to avoid being called a "fiduciary." The Department of Labor issued new "Fiduciary Regulations" in 2017 … but then delayed them … and they were eventually struck down. They would have required advisers to always act in the best interest of their clients with regard to retirement plan assets. Ironically, when the regulators issued this mandate, most Americans asked (and rightfully so) "You mean you have *NOT* been operating in my best interest?"

And the financial industry's response to this heightened burden to "do the right thing" ... was to lobby for an exception and then to eventually get the Regulations thrown out. The lesson from this chapter is to realize not all advisers are always doing what's in our best interest.

Broadly speaking, there are essentially three different models within the financial industry.

1. The captive insurance model.
2. The brokerage firm model.
3. The independent advisory model.

Each of these three models have representatives called "Financial Advisers." This can be confusing because while the names are similar, who they are working for is dramatically different.

The Captives

The financial adviser in a captive investment firm or captive insurance model is working for the captive insurance agency. In fact, the "financial advisers" in this context are reconstituted insurance agents. As the name "captive" implies, they are "captive agents" who are tasked with selling the firm's proprietary products. They may also be incented to sell insurance and annuity products.

These products may be more expensive and may not be appropriate for all of their clients ... but they are not working for their clients ... they are working for the insurance company. Their regulatory burden is only to prove "suitability" rather than to do what is SOLELY in the best interest of their client.

I heard a large insurance company advertisement recently boasting an extremely high client retention rate. The implication, of course, is that clients stay because the insurance is great. But the advertisement is misleading.

The insurance products may be fantastic, but the real reason clients do not leave those captive agencies is because they cannot leave. Other financial advisers at other firms are not allowed to "sell" those insurance policies. In other words, if a person buys an insurance policy (or annuity) from a captive insurance agent, and then later decides they want to work with a different financial adviser, it is not possible to move their policy to a different adviser (from outside the captive). The only way to leave the captive agency is to cancel or surrender the policy. And most clients do not abandon their policy. Hence, the insurance company has an extremely high retention rate.

The captive agents are also "held captive" because they are selling a proprietary product. If they ever decided to leave the agency they would have to leave all of their clients and policies behind and start over.

In a captive agency, the policies are held captive, the agents are held captive, and sometimes the clients may feel like they too are held captive.

The Brokers

The brokerage firm model is more flexible, in the sense that brokers are not held captive to any particular insurance company or investment product. Technically, a financial adviser who is a broker can sell any financial product to their client … unless it is owned by a captive insurance company that only allows it to be sold by their agents.

If a person is seeking a pilot for their retirement plan, hiring a broker as their financial adviser means they are hiring a salesman who makes their living "brokering" deals. Many brokers are good people and many of them are able to "broker" or sell great products. It should be understood, though, that a financial adviser who is a broker is not selling advice, they are selling financial products. They are not in the business of giving advice; they are in the business of brokering a deal or trading investments.

To be clear, there is nothing wrong with this business model, if it is properly disclosed and the client completely understands for whom the financial adviser is really working. If I needed an insurance policy, for instance, I might contact a broker. But if I needed financial advice, I would not contact a broker.

Disclosure is the key. The analogy often used is from the medical community. Would we want to see a doctor who was paid to sell certain drugs? They might be the best drugs on the market, but an arrangement between the pharmaceutical company and the doctor would appear to be a conflict of interest.

A financial adviser working for a captive or working for a brokerage firm is likely a Registered Representative (typically called a Registered Rep). This means they are paid commission for selling investment products or insurance products. The pilot's check is their commission check, and it fluctuates based upon what they sell.

Brokers work for the commission check. A broker needs a "broker-dealer" (sometimes referred to as a "wirehouse,"[12] particularly if it references one of the "big four" Wall Street firms which serve as broker-dealers).[13]

To be clear, brokers have their place. I use brokers, when looking to "broker" a trade. But I do not ask brokers for advice.

The Independents

The third general option is the independent advisory model. Rather than the commission-based insurance model, this is the fee-based fiduciary model. The financial advisers in this model are called Investment Advisor Representatives, and their firm is called a Registered Investment Advisor.

Brokers need Broker-Dealers or BDs; independent advisors need Registered Investment Advisors or RIAs. The BDs report to the Financial Industry Regulatory Authority (FINRA). RIAs report to the U.S. Securities and Exchange Commission (SEC). FINRA is an independent, nongovernmental organization. The SEC is an independent agency of the United States federal government.

The financial advisor in the Independent model is not paid commission on each transaction or trade, so there is no incentive for them to make trades that do not benefit their clients. A financial advisor in the RIA model is paid an advisory fee by the client, their business is investment advice, and they are held to a "fiduciary standard," legally obligated to do what is SOLELY in the best interest of their clients.

This might seem like a "no-brainer" (that the advisor would have to do what is in the best interest of the clients) but the financial advisors in the other models have a "suitability" standard, only required to determine if the particular investment is suitable for the client before selling it.

The financial advisor in this third model is paid an advisory fee as either an asset-based fee or a flat fee. If paid a percentage of assets (an asset-based fee) the financial advisor has an incentive to grow the assets in the account because if the assets go up their income also increases. But sometimes a financial advisor will simply charge a flat fee for holistic financial advice, providing direction on a client's entire financial picture. This type of service goes beyond simply managing the money within a particular account. For a flat fee this financial adviser can actually give unbiased investment advice.

For example, if I meet with a financial adviser who is advising me and my wife on our entire financial picture, the adviser might say, "Based on my assessment you are under-insured. You need to buy more life insurance." It may, in fact, be true that I am underinsured, but if, in the next breath, the adviser pulls out her insurance card and says, "Oh, by the way, I also sell insurance," I might reasonably suspect her motives for advising me to buy more insurance were not completely pure. Maybe they were. Maybe they weren't. But clearly there is a conflict of interest.

If, instead, the financial adviser who suggests I am underinsured does not herself sell insurance, the "advice" appears to be more objective.

If I am paying an independent advisor at an RIA a flat fee for financial advice, I can expect to receive unadulterated, unbiased advice. And the advice, in some instances, might be to contact a broker to buy an insurance product.

- Call an independent adviser for advice.
- Call a broker to buy a particular product.
- Call a captive if the product is sold by the captive agency.

Whether it is independent or captive, commission-based or fee-only, they each have their place. The point in seeking the right "pilot" is to understand who a person is hiring, and who the pilot will be working for, and what the client is trying to accomplish.

A person can know the model of a particular pilot by looking at their disclosures, the language that has to appear at the bottom of the advisor's emails, stationary, business cards, and website. It will either reference "Registered Investment Advisor" (which is the third model) or it will say "Securities offered through _____" and possibly indicate that the organization is a member of FINRA/SIPC. This is an indication they are operating in one of the first two models. (NOTE: It is also common that some financial advisers operate in a "hybrid" model, meaning they can work as both a fee-based adviser and a commission-based broker. If they are wearing their fee-based hat they are working for the client, but if they are wearing their broker hat they are working for commissions.)

My advice

My advice is to understand these three models, do some research, and interview several potential pilots. A person should not hire the first pilot they find, regardless of how well they know them. They should always get a second opinion.

Part of the interviewing and due diligence should be using the information regulators make available as a matter of public record. Financial advisers are required to disclose any customer complaints, any regulatory violations, any lawsuits (even if the suit was settled in the adviser's favor), and any irregularities. If an adviser filed for bankruptcy, or if an adviser is in trouble with the IRS and has a tax lien, or if there are or were ever any criminal charges, they are required by law to disclose those to the public.

There are many outstanding professionals in the financial industry who have completely clean records, but there are others who continue to have issues. Unfortunately, they also continue to be hired because people fail to conduct a background check before hiring them to pilot their ship.

FINRA provides information at **https://brokercheck.finra.org/** about financial advisers operating in one of the first two models (as a broker or as a captive insurance agent).

The SEC provides info at **https://www.adviserinfo.sec.gov/** about their advisors.

A person should check out the pilots before handing over the controls, paying particular attention to the sections on these websites titled "Disclosures."

My advice is to do the homework, interview several advisers, and do a background check.

If hiring a Fee-only advisor, a person needs to be prepared to pay them a flat fee to manage their finances. Some plan participants to whom I suggest this cringe at the idea of paying a flat fee upfront for financial advice, but if it is not a flat fee the financial adviser may be making money through underlying commissions which may cost more than the flat fee.

Piloting is not free, nor should it be.

Self-pilotage can be very costly but hiring the wrong pilot could be costly through commissions and hidden fees.

A person can get a second opinion to make sure the fee is fair, but if they are not paying a fee a person should wonder if the advisor is working for them or the commission check, if they have their best interest at heart or if the particular product they are offering fulfills some sell order they were given at the office.

Beyond this, my over-arching advice is to find an adviser who has a teacher's heart, and a heart for understanding each person's unique goals, and a heart for Repurposement. We each need a pilot who is our advocate, who wants to steer the ship in the direction of our heart's desire.

Take the search for a pilot seriously. It's a big decision. Give it some thought, prayerful consideration, and time.

If the ship enters the port and is still flying the flag that says "I require a pilot" ... the journey will not end well.

Having the right pilot is key to finishing the journey and key to making sure a person finishes the journey in the right port (a function of Repurposement and living on purpose).

As Seneca said, "If a man knows not what harbor he seeks, any wind is the right wind."[14]

1. This may be changing with younger generations now entering the workforce who grew up shopping online, but it does not change my advice to test drive retirement before buying.

2. According to a Deutsche Bank report issued November, 2018

3. J.P. Morgan Asset Management, Guide to Retirement 2019 Edition, pages 13-14.

4. Ibid.

5. Ibid.

6. Ibid.

7. According to the EBRI Retirement Security Projection Model® (RSPM) developed in 2003, as of 2019. www.ebri.org

8. In some cases, 30% of your income could exceed the contribution limits the plan and/or the IRS allows. If this is the case, it might require some additional creativity and discipline, like investing the extra amount in a savings account without the added tax benefits. The point is to try to not touch it during this trial period.)

9. "Review and Analysis of Harbor Pilot Net Revenues and Salary Levels," West Gulf Maritime Association. Some readers who are thinking of repurposing may be sensing a "call" to park boats. It is very lucrative.

10. I am a Certified Plan Fiduciary Advisor (CPFA®) meaning I am certified to be a fiduciary and to advise the plan fiduciaries (the employers who sponsor 401k plans).

11. "Misbehaving: The Making of Behavioral Economics," Richard Thaler, 2015. P. 52.

12. The term "wirehouse" owes its origins to the fact that, prior to the advent of modern wireless communications, brokerage firms were connected to their branches primarily through telephone and telegraph wires. This enabled branches to have access to the same market information as the head office, thus allowing their brokers to provide stock quotes and market news to their clients, according to www.investopedia.com.

13. The four largest and most well-known wirehouse full-service brokerage firms today are Morgan Stanley, Bank of America's Merrill Lynch, UBS, and Wells Fargo, as of Jul 18, 2018, according to www.investopedia.com.)

14. This advice was from Lucius Annaeus Seneca (a.k.a. Seneca the Younger, 4 BC–65 AD). It is also translated as, "When a man does not know what harbour he is making for, no wind is the right wind." — Seneca the Younger, *Letter LXXI: On the supreme good*, line 3.)

Taking Off ...

The Flight Path For A Healthy Retirement Plan

Hover over an airplane to reveal the plan

CRUISE

CLIMB

PREPARING TO LAND

TAKEOFF

LAND

From www.PlanHealthDesign.com

Takeoff - What are the defaults for the retirement plan, and are they set to help or harm the objective of helping you retire better? We'd hate for the plane to take off without you and leave you grounded. Our team excels in getting everybody on board

Climb - The participants in a retirement plan don't just automatically climb towards their retirement goals unless there is an intentional and purposeful effort to facilitate the process. If fees are excessive, if contributions are low, or if the communication and guidance in the Break Room is not on target, the gravitational pull will prevent success.

Cruise - The participants in a retirement plan have the opportunity to set the flight to cruise control once they reach their cruising altitude, meaning proper diversification and rebalancing of their account occurs as they move along a customized glide-path. We like to assist each employee with finding their own customized portfolio and glide-path, a combination of their risk tolerance and their retirement target date, knowing that using cruise control should mean less turbulence over the course of the journey and should promote better long-term success.

The Flight Path For A Healthy Retirement Plan

Hover over an airplane to reveal the plan

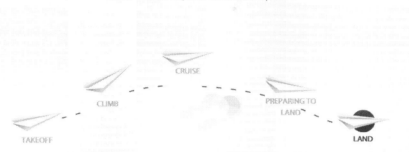

From www.PlanHealthDesign.com

Preparing to Land - The closer a participant gets to the end of their journey the greater the importance of customized personal guidance. Have they considered where they'd like to land, and when they can land, and how much fuel they need to land? Have they factored into the equation Social Security and ongoing health care needs? It will be important to sit down with a Financial Planner for in-depth planning, a trusted planner who embodies a teacher's heart and a servant mindset. Finding the right pilot is key.

Land - With so much attention on the accumulation process in retirement, we feel like there is far too little focus on the distribution process, but how a participant lands is crucial. It would be a shame to successfully pilot the plane through retirement only to crash at the end of the journey. A proper landing is vital to success and there is nothing automatic about the process. A successful landing may not mean wasting money on an annuity where fees can erode years of hard work. We don't believe a person needs insurance for their money, but they do need to think carefully and purposefully about how to land.

CONCLUSION
CHOOSING REPURPOSEMENT
Repurposement as the key to Happiness & Longevity

This book is about making the 401(k) work, for getting the most out of the greatest and most reliable vehicle for building wealth.

It starts with keeping it 'simple and clear': replacing confusing investment classes and retirement education with the foundational blocks of 'How Much' and 'Where' (and the emphasis on 'How Much' as the largest contributor to success). It proceeds from 'simple and clear' to a holistic and compassionate approach to financial wellness, helping employees manage their resources so they can invest enough to be successful. But the key is to understand the 'why', to start with the why, and couch the simple and clear message and holistic financial wellness within an invitation that is compelling.

I believe the 401(k) works when we are captured by a vision for Repurposement.

I also believe behavioral change happens at the intersection of 'simple and clear,' 'holistic and compassionate' and 'compelling and motivating.' The 401(k) doesn't just work without some concerted effort and cost on our part.

To borrow from the example used in Chapter 4, the greatest 'cost' of the 401(k) is really an opportunity cost. An investment of $416.67 a month ($5,000 a year and $200,000 over a 40-year career) could net a million-dollar return. The 'cost' of the 401(k) is not $416.67 a month but an opportunity cost of $1,000,000.[1]

Keep in mind, the average monthly car loan payment in the U.S. is $554 on new vehicles and $391 on used vehicles.[2] An investor could put $416.67 a month into a car, a depreciating asset worth less over time, or into a retirement vehicle worth more over time. Some American workers struggle to invest this much in the 401(k) but have little trouble investing this much in a car loan.

The 401(k) is not complicated … but it's also not easy.

In fact, it's hard, it involves tough choices, discipline, patience, and a stick-to-itiveness we don't often see in our culture. It seems like most people are looking for easy, quick results, but the odds are strongly against success with this approach. The 401(k), on the other hand, is a proven method of building wealth. It just takes a small, consistent, long-term investment. It's not easy, and there are many ways to mess this us. Some start too late, some invest too little, some don't have the patience or fortitude to stick with it, and some even sabotage their own accounts with pre-retirement distributions or loans.

But the ones who stick with it receive enormous rewards.

And for those who say they can't afford to stick with it, remember that this is the opportunity to be a millionaire for less than the cost of the average new car payment.[3]

The 401(k) is not a tool for the rich, a perk for the '1%' to get richer. In fact, according to the American Retirement Association, nearly three-quarters of 401(k) participants earn less than $100,000 and a third earn less than $50,000. The 401(k) is not for rich people. The 401(k) is for average Americans who want to stop being average.

But it's all about choices.

And when a person gets to the end of the journey, after putting on a ton of miles, they have one more choice to make.

Repurpose, recycle, or retire?

Repurposed materials can have a great second life, a second application, so to speak. And similarly, every person has the opportunity to be redeemed and repurposed.

But it is their choice.

And the choice starts much earlier than most people might imagine. The choice starts long before the tread on our tires wears thin, before the odometer reads 50,000 miles, before the check engine line is screaming at us.

The choice starts when the newly-hired kid is given an enrollment form at work and asked to make the largest financial decision of their lives. And the choice starts with every good financial decision along the journey, every decision to manage money rather than be managed by it. And the choice starts with tough decisions to not acquiesce to debt. A person living beyond their means now and ill-prepared for the future will later have fewer choices because they will have a limited band of options they can afford.

The choice starts today.

Regardless of what yesterday held, today is the first day of the rest of your life. It's your choice what to make of it.

The choices we make from today forward will affect not only our life, but also our legacy.

America is facing a retirement crisis, mortgaging the future by continuing to roll the snowball of our money problems forward. The risk for employees in not facing this crisis is having to continue punching the clock at a job they hate beyond their expected retirement date. And the risk to employers in not having people retirement ready is keeping them on the payroll too long, beyond their most productive years, as healthcare costs continue to rise.

No one denies there's a retirement crisis, but many disagree on the nature and solution to the problem. I believe the problem stems from aiming at the wrong thing: checking out to a meaningless existence in retirement. And I believe the solution requires a paradigm shift: investing and stewarding resources to provide the financial freedom to be repurposed on your timetable.

After all, having enough money to stop being productive may not be a blessing.

Some kids who grow up tremendously wealthy grow up without the need to produce. It may sound like a blessing for their needs to be provided, but the blessing can be a curse if there is no need to create or produce a purposeful living.

Some adults invest so well when working they get to a point in retirement savings where they need not produce another dime. Quite literally, their money is making enough money (through investments) that they need not make any more money.

But leaving an occupation which gave them purpose for a purposeless retirement devoid of structure and meaning can be a curse. Bored and unproductive, some retirees die too soon while studies continue to show those who work longer live longer. The Roman statesman Marcus Tullius Cicero would not be a fan of what retirement has become in our age. He wrote that the best antidote to aging was a purposeful life. "I am in my eighty-fourth year yet, as you see, old age has not quite unnerved or shattered me. The senate and the popular assembly never find my vigor wanting." Cicero, of course, was one of the greatest speech writers in history, work he found purposeful and life-giving until his final days. And as a wielder of the pen and not the plow, his age was an asset in experience rather than a liability that a more physically-taxing job might have been.[4]

What if the retirement years are just an opportunity to work more creatively, maybe a chance to work for free if we invested enough and don't need the income, but to continue creating, producing and contributing to society? Perhaps creating is the gift which keeps on giving, giving to the world around us and giving us a reason to keep waking up each morning.

The mother-load of happiness – striking it rich – is finding significance in something greater than ourselves, like what we produce. If it is not bigger than us or greater than us or worthy of our legacy, it is not worthy of our investment.

Many people will testify that their 'second act' was their most fulfilling, the greatest source of happiness. Whether it's Oscar-nominated actor Gene Hackman as a novelist, President George W. Bush as a painter, or Microsoft founder Bill Gates as a philanthropist, the encore can be quite fulfilling.

William Shakespeare, the greatest playwright of his day, and perhaps of any day, wrote many 'acts' for the stage … but a 2019 film, "All is True," speculates how his final act might have been the worst of tragedies. The film is set in 1613, when Shakespeare is established as the greatest author of his day. But when his Globe Theatre burns to the ground he decides to retire, and his version of retirement is pure hell. Each day he putters in his garden, cursing Mother Nature; each night he returns home to be cursed by his family, haunted by the death of his only son. It's a depressing picture, but it's not unlike the picture some have of retirement. 'What now?' they ask, as each day melts into the next.

The second act can be fulfilling and purposeful … or it can feel like being put out to pasture. And if a person's picture of the future is the latter, like the second act of Shakespeare, it's no wonder they lack the motivation to properly prepare.

Too many Americans suffer from extreme procrastination, but maybe it's because the vision of the future isn't inspiring enough. It's like they are on the Titanic, they see the iceberg looming, but they choose to go back below deck and continue the party. They know they should prepare for the future, and they intend to do so … someday.

Someday may be one of the most dangerous words in the English language.

Someday I'm going to get my financial house in order. Someday I'll figure out the work-life balance thing, I'll prioritize the really important things in life, like my family and my health. Someday I'll start investing in the future. Someday I'll put my budget on paper. Someday I'll tackle my credit card debt.

Someday.

Someday when we have kids and increase our insurance policy;

Someday when the kids start school we'll start a college fund;

Someday when the kids leave home and we downsize;

Someday when the kids graduate from college and we help them pay off their college debt;

Someday when I hit forty-five ... or fifty-five;

I'm going to start taking the 401(k) seriously.

Someday.

But someday never comes. Or it comes too late.

Someday is today, not tomorrow.

Edgar Albert Guest wrote a poem entitled **Tomorrow**.[5]

He was going to be all that a mortal should be ... Tomorrow.
No one should be kinder or braver than he ... Tomorrow.
A friend who was troubled and weary he knew,
Who'd be glad of a lift and who needed it, too;
On him he would call and see what he could do ... Tomorrow.

Each morning he stacked up the letters he'd write ... Tomorrow.
And thought of the folks he would fill with delight ... Tomorrow.
It was too bad, indeed, he was busy today,
And hadn't a minute to stop on his way;
More time he would have to give others, he'd say ... Tomorrow.

The greatest of workers this man would have been ... Tomorrow.
The world would have known him, had he ever seen ... Tomorrow.
But the fact is he died and he faded from view,
And all that he left here when living was through
Was a mountain of things he intended to do ... Tomorrow.

There are no guarantees about tomorrow, about how long we'll live or how much money we may need. But Repurposement is about making the most of every day. Repurposement is not about how much money we'll make. Repurposement is about how much of an impact we'll make.

The choice is yours.

I hope we don't keep waiting too long for *someday* to get our financial house in order or tomorrow may never come… or it may come too soon.

The time to start repurposing is not tomorrow.

The time to start is today.

1. Again, as further elaborated in Chapter 4, this illustration from Source of data: J.P. Morgan Asset Management assumes an annual contribution of $5,000 invested every year from age 25 to age 65, in a diversified portfolio that grows at a compounding rate of return of 7%.
2. This was the average monthly car payment in the first quarter of 2019, according to Experian data, as of June 27, 2019.
3. Ibid.
4. This quote is from his essay, "Cato the Elder on Aging." Cicero lived by the pen, but he died by the sword, murdered on the command of Mark Antony for having written speeches on behalf of Mark Antony's opponents in the Roman Republic.
5. Edgar Allen Guest, known as Eddie Guest, was an English-born American poet who was popular in the first half of the 20th century and became known as the People's Poet. Born in Birmingham, England in 1881, his family moved to Michigan when he was a child. In 1895, he started working as a journalist for the Detroit Free Press. In addition to his stories, most editions of the Free Press also ran one of his poems. 'Tomorrow' was published there in 1942.

AFTERWORD

A personal note about finding a Pilot

In Chapter 9 we discussed finding a pilot for the retirement plan vehicle, the fact that many ports have compulsory pilotage requiring a ship's captain to surrender the piloting of their vessel to someone familiar with those waters, but that in many areas of life there is not compulsory pilotage.

Pilotage is not required for the biggest decisions in life.

I believe a person needs multiple 'pilots' in their life to be healthy, and there is a direct correlation between the degree of 'self-piloting' and unhealthiness. In maritime jargon, the signal flag G is supposed to be flown as a ship enters a port. It simply means, 'I require a pilot.'

It's a cry for help and many of us should be flying this flag.

My friend, Jimmy Dodd, once mentioned to me there are at least six roles everyone needs filled in their lives to be healthy. He broke them down as three personal roles and three professional roles. He said everyone needs a mentor, a counselor and a friend (those are the personal roles) and everyone needs a boss, a trainer and a coach (those are the professional roles). These six 'pilots' can keep us on course. And I can testify from experience that when these roles are not filled it is not healthy.

For example, even though I own my own firm, I do not work for myself. I work for my clients. If I forget they're my 'boss' ...they may not be clients long. I am accountable to them, as I am accountable to my family, as I am accountable to my employees and their families.

The point of this book is to emphasize the importance of having a pilot for the retirement plan and being purposeful about writing the next chapter of your life. But I would be remiss if I failed to mention that I also believe we need a spiritual pilot.

Self-piloting will eventually leave us shipwrecked.

I was in college when I first understood the need for a Pilot. I was (and I still am) the captain of my own ship, but I allowed the Pilot to come aboard and take control of the wheel. This Pilot, of course, is God. I figured the Creator of this vessel was better skilled at piloting than I was, that the Author who started this story should write the next chapter.

I will confess that for me personally it has been an interesting journey through often congested waters, and that the path has not always been smooth (although looking back I realize the rockiest legs of the journey, the choppiest waters that I had to traverse, were the segments of the trip where I tried to wrestle the piloting back into my control). Successful pilotage requires a daily, almost hourly, surrendering to the Pilot of my ship, because I am still the captain and still capable, at any point, of taking back control and shipwrecking this vessel.

I've done this a few times too.

Part of what has made it interesting and challenging for me was the confusion over my identify. When I submitted to God's *pilotage*, I immediately began serving in ministry (i.e., doing ministry as a job). The line between who I was (or whose I was) was blurred with what I did. Many years later, when I felt called to the second chapter of my life (the retirement plan industry) I would describe the transition as one fraught with a bit of an identity crisis. It was, and has been, a journey for me to understand my identity has not changed (just my job). My identity is the same as when the pilotage started: I'm *still* His kid; He's still my Father; I'm still called to serve others.

Turns out God was more interested in me than what I did anyway. And knowing this makes it so much easier to submit to the coaching, guidance, expertise and care of the Pilot of my soul.

But it is not *compulsory pilotage*. A person can pilot their own vessel just like they can pilot their own 401(k). We're the captain. We get to choose the pilot.

My advice is to not be your own pilot. If you are still serving as both captain and pilot, I would urge you to reconsider this strategy.

I welcome questions about finding a pilot for the 401(k) or a Pilot for life. Let's start a dialogue. Visit the website for this book: https://www.planhealthdesign.com/repurposement/ or email me directly: troy@PHDfirm.com

ACKNOWLEDGMENTS

- Photographs of the author: Linsey McAfee.
- "Repurposement" – I first heard the term from Matt Syverson. It captured my heart and I ran with it, though I repurposed the term in a slightly different fashion. Matt Syverson also believes he heard the term somewhere else ... though he can't remember where. While neither of us invented the term, both of us have repurposed it.
- "The evilness of averages" was a term I borrowed from Robert Cruz, though he too borrowed it from somewhere else.
- "Practice Retirement" is a concept inspired by Peter Dunn (aka 'Pete the Planner') though he calls it "Mock Retirement."
- A special thanks to the hospitality of the monks at Conception Abbey throughout this process. I discovered the monastery provided the best way to get away (from the office, technology, email and phones) while remaining connected to the Author.
- And my heartfelt gratitude to a team of editors and friends who provided invaluable feedback throughout this process, first from within my inner circle, and eventually with the team at Walsworth. Thanks to Kristalynn, Matt, Brian, Paul, Tom, Mercedes, John, and Chet. Could not have done this without you.

To my knowledge, the other stories and illustrations fell out of my own head. But I will say, I have told and retold some of these stories so many times that I can't honestly recall when I first thought of them. It is entirely possible some of them were heard or overheard somewhere else, or some iteration of them was told by someone else, and then they became part of my story. I once heard an illustration about anecdotal attribution that is pertinent. The story goes like this:

- The first few times I share a story, I say, "So-and-so told me this..."
- The next few times I share the story, I say, "I've heard it said..."
- But eventually when I share the story, I say, "As I've always said..." because in telling and retelling an illustration, it becomes my story.

By the way, I'm not sure who originally said this about anecdotal attributions... it was probably me... at least that's what I've always said.

ABOUT THE AUTHOR

Troy Redstone is a Fee-Only retirement plan consultant, an accomplished public speaker and published author, and Behavioral Finance expert. He designs and manages financial wellness programs and ERISA, employer-sponsored retirement plans (401k, 403b, Governmental 457 plans). He is a Certified Plan Fiduciary Advisor (CPFA®), a Certified

Behavioral Finance Analyst (CBFA®), a Certified Financial Education Instructor (CFEI®), and an Accredited Investment Fiduciary (AIF®).

As the founder of PHD. Retirement Consulting, he helps employees retire better and helps employers sleep better. Known as "The Dave Ramsey of 401k's", he's passionate about promoting financial wellness through retirement plans and encouraging employees to eliminate debt and practice good stewardship.

He is a member of the **Retirement Advisor Council**, recognized as one of the 125 leaders in the retirement plan industry in America, and currently serves on the Board (2018-2020); Chairman of the Board for the **Employee Benefits Institute** (2019); a thought leader in the retirement plan industry; and a thirty-year veteran of keynote speaking at conferences and seminars throughout the country.

He has published articles in a variety of magazines and newspapers including *The Miami Herald*, the *Vero Beach Press Journal* and *The Today Paper*. He attended The University of Alabama (Behavioral Psychology and Journalism), Anderson University (M.Div.) and Rockhurst University (Finance).

He lives in Kansas City with his bride of 25 years; his daughter, the equestrian, when home from college; his high school son, the musician; and an Aussiedoodle named Dixie Belle.

Made in the USA
Columbia, SC
09 April 2020

90068235R00102